NOW YOU KNOW

Baseball

Doug Lennox

DUNDURN PRESS
TORONTO

Project Editor: Michael Carroll
Editor: Barry Jowett
Copy Editor: Jennifer McKnight
Design: Courtney Horner
Printer: Webcom

Library and Archives Canada Cataloguing in Publication

Lennox, Doug
         Now you know baseball / Doug Lennox.

ISBN 978-1-55488-713-2

         1. Baseball--Miscellanea. I. Title.

GV873.L46 2010   796.35702   C2009-907455-9

1   2   3   4   5   14   13   12   11   10

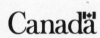

Conseil des Arts   Canada Council
du Canada   for the Arts

ONTARIO ARTS COUNCIL
CONSEIL DES ARTS DE L'ONTARIO

We acknowledge the support of **The Canada Council for the Arts** and the **Ontario Arts Council** for our publishing program. We also acknowledge the financial support of the **Government of Canada** through the **Book Publishing Industry Development Program** and **The Association for the Export of Canadian Books,** and the **Government of Ontario** through the **Ontario Book Publishers Tax Credit program,** and the **Ontario Media Development Corporation.**

Care has been taken to trace the ownership of copyright material used in this book. The author and the publisher welcome any information enabling them to rectify any references or credits in subsequent editions.

J. Kirk Howard, President

Printed and bound in Canada.
Printed on recycled paper.

www.dundurn.com

Dundurn Press
3 Church Street, Suite 500
Toronto, Ontario, Canada
M5E 1M2

Gazelle Book Services Limited
White Cross Mills
High Town, Lancaster, England
LA1 4XS

Dundurn Press
2250 Military Road
Tonawanda, NY
U.S.A. 14150

NOW YOU KNOW

KNOW

Baseball

contents

preface

One of the most remarkable things about baseball is that it is followed passionately by people who are polar opposites. It's a sport that is loved by poets and statisticians. W.P. Kinsella takes us into fantasy worlds in his novels and short stories, making ghosts, time travel, and prophecy seem not just plausible, but factual. On the other side of the brain, Bill James can examine every minutiae of the game with numeric analysis that convinces legions that anything that happens in the game can have a formula applied to it.

Baseball is also loved by both rich and developing nations. The United States and Japan play and watch baseball with a passion. That passion is equalled or surpassed by nations such as the Dominican Republic.

What is it that draws people to this sport? Perhaps it's that the game can be so simple, while at the same time so complex. Or maybe it's the fact that it differs so much from the other major team sports, nearly all of which are played on rectangular playing surfaces and involve moving an object from one end to the other in order to score in a net or other designated area. Baseball is played on a field that fans out from home plate. The defence controls the ball, and the ball never does the scoring — the players themselves do the scoring, and they do so by running a route that brings them back to where they started. And as Kinsella points out, it's a game about infinity: in theory, a game can continue forever as long as no team holds the lead at the end of an extra inning, or a third out is never recorded in the last inning; and when played on a field without an outfield wall, the foul lines are never ending.

Whatever the appeal, baseball fans are attracted to every nuance of their chosen sport, and that's why we have such an insatiable appetite for stories and facts about the game. From rattling off statistics to telling anecdotes about players and games we've seen or heard about, every fan delights in the ongoing history of baseball.

This book is a small part of that ongoing history. One book can't hope to capture all the questions and answers that baseball can inspire, but it is my hope that it captures some of the spirit that the game arouses.

baseball history

Who is the only person to have been home plate umpire and pitcher for no-hitters?

Bill Dineen's career 170–177 record does little to suggest the flashes of brilliance in his career, which included three wins as pitcher for the Red Sox in the 1903 World Series. His best game as a pitcher was a no-hitter hurled against the Chicago White Sox on September 27, 1905.

As an umpire, Dineen had a fantastic reputation, and over the course of his lengthy career he was umpire during five no-hitters. While other people have pitched or umpired no-hitters, Dineen is the only individual to have pitched a no-hitter and served as home plate umpire.

Dineen's no-hitter history includes one notorious event. On June 23, 1917, Dineen was working third base. Red Sox pitcher Babe Ruth walked the first batter of the game. Furious at the call of the home plate umpire, Ruth punched the umpire and was thrown out of the game. Ernie Shore replaced Ruth and retired every batter he faced — Ruth was credited with being part of a combined no-hitter, despite not having recorded a single out.

Who was the first black player in major league baseball?

While Jackie Robinson is the man who broke baseball's shameful colour barrier, he was not the first African-American to play in the major leagues.

Catcher Moses "Fleetwood" Walker was a member of the Toledo Blue Stockings when they joined the American Association (a predecessor of the American League) in 1884. Walker played in only 62 games in an injury-plagued season, and was released at the end of the year.

Others followed Walker, but by the 1900s there were no black players in the major leagues. While the big leagues never had a formal ban, owners adhered to an unwritten rule that prevented African-Americans from playing until 1947, when Dodger General Manager Branch Rickey made the bold move of bringing Jackie Robinson to Brooklyn.

Who applied the "unfavourable chance deviation theory" to baseball?

Though he'd later go on to be a successful manager, winning the World Series with the 1986 Mets, Davey Johnson had a solid career as a player, too. Not only could he play, but he had a brain in his head as well ... though perhaps he over-thought things once in a while. When Orioles pitcher Dave McNally was struggling with his control, Johnson, a former math major, resorted to theories of mathematical probability. "Haven't you ever heard of the unfavourable chance deviation theory?" Johnson asked. "Aim for the middle of the plate when you're wild. The ball will end up in the corners, which is where you want it, anyway."

> **They Said It ...**
> Reporter: "Do you think Ty Cobb is up there looking down at you as you chase the record?"
> Pete Rose: "From what I know about the guy, he may not be up there. He may be down there."

Where was baseball first played?

The origins of baseball are murky at best. While the legend that baseball was invented by Abner Doubleday and first played in Cooperstown, New York, was once the "official" story, it was, alas, baseless. The committee that gave Doubleday and Cooperstown the nod has been accused not of trying to find out where baseball was invented, but of trying to prove that it was invented in the United States.

Various places in the United States and Canada have claimed to be the birthplaces of baseball, but in reality the game developed from a number of bat-and-ball games played in England. In fact, there are many references in British writings to a game called "base-ball" or "baseball." The game is even referenced in Jane Austen's *Northanger Abbey* (written in 1799).

The United States can lay claim to hosting the first *organized* baseball game played between two clubs. On October 6, 1845, the Knickerbocker Club took on the New York Nine at Elysian Fields in Hoboken, New Jersey.

Who was the first black umpire in the majors?

In the history of baseball's integration in the 1940s, 1950s, and 1960s, Emmett Ashford is often overlooked.

"Ash" first made history by becoming the first African-American to umpire in professional baseball when he took the field in the Southwest International League in 1951. There he became known for his exaggerated calls and ritzy wardrobe. But it wasn't until 15 years later, on April 1, 1966, that he got his shot as the first black major league umpire.

Which team played their first game in the snow?

After the National League's successful expansion into Canada with the Montreal Expos in 1969, the American League decided to go international as well, adding the Toronto Blue Jays for the 1977 season.

But the weather seemed to be uncooperative. Snow blanketed the field at Toronto's Exhibition Stadium for the scheduled home opener on April 7. The Blue Jays organization was determined to get the first game in, and the Jays and Chicago White Sox took to the field in weather that may have resulted in a postponement on any other day. The Jays won their franchise opener 9–5 on the strength of two home runs by Doug Ault.

Quickies

Did you know ...

- that the baseball tradition of spring training came about in 1885 when the Chicago White Stockings went to Hot Springs in Arkansas to prepare for the new season?

Who wrote the book *Ball Four*?

It was long assumed that professional athletes engaged in hijinks while on the road, but until Jim Bouton's 1970 book *Ball Four* blew the lid off of ballplayers' not-so-wholesome lifestyle, few knew just how much trouble big leaguers actually got into.

Bouton had been a pitcher for nine seasons from 1962–70 (he later made a comeback bid in 1978), and freely implicated himself while storytelling. *Ball Four* depicted major league players as heavy drinkers and frequently unfaithful to their spouses.

Many players and some owners criticized Bouton for the book. Even some baseball wives were upset with him. Nancy Marshall, wife of pitcher Mike Marshall, said that many wives "didn't want to think about the times when their husbands were on the road, let alone read a story that confirmed their worst suspicions."

> **Quickies**
> *Did you know ...*
> • that in 1910, the cork center was added to the official baseball?

What previously unexplored market did the Detroit Tigers tap into when they signed Gates Brown and Ron LeFlore?

Though signed four years apart, in 1968 and 1972 respectively, it's hard not to think of Gates Brown and Ron LeFlore as part of the same baseball class, since both were picked up by the Detroit Tigers out of prison.

Brown had been serving time in a prison in Ohio for breaking and entering convictions, and he played on the prison baseball team. His coach was so impressed with his abilities that he brought him to the attention of major league scouts. The Tigers eventually signed Brown after a bidding war for his services. Though never a major part of the starting lineup, Gates was strong off the bench, batting .370 off the pines in 1968.

Ron LeFlore was an even bigger success, after his prison years. LeFlore had had drug problems as a youth and was eventually imprisoned after he and a group of friends held up a bar in Detroit, making off with $35,000. While in prison, LeFlore played for the prison ball team, and though he was never a fan of the sport, he excelled. He was given a tryout with the Tigers after another inmate contacted a friend who knew then-Tigers' manager, Billy Martin. LeFlore made the team and proved to be a valuable contributor. Ironically, he was especially adept at stealing bases. He led the league in stolen sacks twice, including 97 swipes in 1980.

How many players have played in both the Little League World Series, the College World Series, and the Major League Baseball World Series?

Only two players have pulled off the unlikely triumvirate of World Series appearances.

Ed Vosberg was the first. Vosberg's Little League World Series performance included a one-hitter in the semi-finals of the 1973 tournament. Later, he was a member of the 1980 NCAA champions, the University of Arizona. Finally, he pitched three innings of relief for the Florida Marlins in the 1997 World Series.

The other veteran of the three different World Series is Jason Varitek. His Little League World Series performance was less impressive — he went zero for seven in 1984. He later helped Georgia Tech win the 1994 College World Series. As a pro, he was part of the curse-breaking 2004 World Championship won by the Boston Red Sox.

Varitek actually did Vosberg one better; in addition to the three World Series, he also played on the U.S. team in the 1992 Olympics.

How long was the 1989 World Series delayed by the Bay Area earthquake?

The 1989 season was an unhappy one for baseball. It was the year that Pete Rose was banned for life and commissioner Bart Giamatti died suddenly of a heart attack. But the misfortune that befell the World Series that year went far beyond baseball — a massive earthquake rocked the San Francisco Bay area, killing 63 people and injuring thousands.

The scope of the disaster made the disruption of the series — which featured the two Bay Area teams, the San Francisco Giants and the Oakland Athletics — a minor inconvenience.

The quake occurred during the opening ceremonies of Game 3 on October 17, and forced the suspension of the series. Play resumed 10 days later, on October 27. The Athletics went on to sweep — the only World Series win for a team that many thought had "dynasty" written all over it.

How many times did the Brooklyn Dodgers and the New York Yankees meet in the World Series?

World Series showdowns between the Brooklyn Dodgers and New York Yankees were starting to feel like annual events in the 1940s and 1950s, with the Yankees having the better of the Dodgers year after year before the Bums finally triumphed in 1955.

In the history of the rivalry, the two teams faced each other in the Series seven times: 1941, 1947, 1949, 1952, 1953, 1955, and 1956. In fact, aside from appearances in the Fall Classic in 1916 and 1920 (at a time when the team was known as the Robins), the Brooklyn squad never played a World Series against a team other than the Yankees.

After the Dodgers moved to Los Angeles, the teams did not meet in October again until 1963. They later renewed their rivalry in three memorable World Series confrontations in 1977, 1978, and 1981.

Who was the first team to have a permanent spring training home?

Spring training had existed since the 19th century, but teams would generally move around from state to state, and sometimes their spring training would take place near (or even in) the city they represented in the regular season.

While spring training is, nowadays, played in Grapefruit League (Florida) or

Quickies
Did you know ...

- that in the 1890s, American baseball teams played soccer in the off-season in order to keep their stadiums operating through the winter months? Often the same players who were on the baseball teams would also play soccer. The first American soccer championship was won by the moonlighting Baltimore Orioles of baseball's National League. (Not the same Orioles who would later become the New York Yankees.)

Cactus League (Arizona) locations, the first "permanent" spring training base was the New York Giants' camp in Marlin Springs, Texas. The Giants trained there from 1908 to 1918.

Why did the Seattle Pilots only last one season?

Long before the Mariners entered the American League in 1977, the Seattle Pilots got the city on the Major League map in the 1969 season. The Pilots were one of four expansion franchises that year, the others being the San Diego Padres and Montreal Expos in the National League, and the Kansas City Royals in the American League.

The Pilots were rushed into existence. The original plan was that they, and their expansion partners, would not play until 1971, but folks in Missouri — particularly Senator Stuart Symington — were making noise about scrapping baseball's antitrust exemption. They were hot over the decision to allow the Kansas City Athletics to move to Oakland, and weren't prepared to wait two years.

So, the Royals — and the Expos, Padres, and Pilots — began life in 1969. The Pilots were not financially prepared, nor did they have an adequate stadium. Their home field was a converted minor league facility that seated 17,000 fans. Worse, they were barely able to cover the expansion fee.

Though they outdrew four other major league teams, their attendance was woeful and it was clear the Pilots would not last long enough for a new domed stadium to be built. So, when a group led by Bud Selig emerged with a plan to buy the Pilots and move them to Wisconsin, the nail was in the coffin for Seattle baseball for the time being, and the Milwaukee Brewers were born.

Which team played out of two home stadiums in 2003 and 2004?

The Montreal Expos had been struggling to bring in crowds for years, particularly since the 1994 strike put an end to a season in which the

Expos seemed destined for the postseason and were thought by many to be poised for a World Series run. By 2003, the state of the team was dire, and Major League Baseball had assumed ownership.

With Expos fans already pointing fingers at MLB for the team's woes, baseball decided that the Expos would have two homes for the 2003 season, and would play 22 games out of San Juan, Puerto Rico.

The arrangement continued in the 2004 season, which would ultimately be the team's last as a representative of Montreal. In 2005, the Expos became the Washington Nationals — though to this day, Expos fans refer to the team not-so-lovingly as "the Gnats."

Who were the division leaders when the 1994 season was halted by a strike?

One way or another, 1994 was destined to become a historic season for major league baseball. It was the first season with six divisions, and three rounds of playoffs were planned.

The postseason never arrived, however, as a players' strike ended the season on August 11. The playoffs and World Series were scrapped.

The sudden end to the season was most keenly felt by fans of the teams that had playoff hopes, and in particular, the division leaders. The New York Yankees (AL East) and Montreal Expos (NL East) were the class of baseball, and held commanding leads in their divisions (six and a half and six games respectively). The Chicago White Sox held a one game lead in the new AL Central, while the Texas Rangers were also up by one in the AL West.

Notable Moments in the Early Days of Baseball

1845: The rules of baseball are developed by Alexander Joy Cartwright.

1846: The Knickerbockers and a group of cricket players play the first "official" game of baseball.

1867: The first (known) curveball in baseball is thrown by Candy Cummings.

1869: An all-professional team, the Cincinnati Red Stockings, takes the field for the first time.

1876: The National League is created.

1882: The American Baseball Association is established.

1889: The Players' League is created.

1900: The American League is created.

1903: The first World Series is played between the Boston Pilgrims and the Pittsburgh Pirates.

The Cincinatti Reds led the NL Central by a slim half game, and the Los Angeles Dodgers were up three and a half games in the NL West.

Teams leading their divisions at the time of the strike were named division champions. The previous year's league champions — the Philadelphia Phillies and Toronto Blue Jays — were listed as reigning league champions going into the next season, and the Jays as reigning World Champions.

Who had the best record in baseball in 1981, but failed to make the playoffs?

The 1981 season was marred by the first-ever midseason players' strike. Players walked out in June and didn't return until August.

Rather than simply continuing the season with the playoff races that were in progress at the time of the strike, owners decided to split the season in two: teams leading their divisions when the strike began were automatically awarded playoff spots, while teams leading their divisions at season's end would also make the playoffs, and there would be an extra round to determine division champions.

This worked out nicely for the teams that earned playoff spots, but for the St. Louis Cardinals and Cincinnati Reds, it was a travesty. The Cardinals' overall record in the 1981 season was the best in the NL East, and yet, because they finished second to two different teams in each half, they missed the playoffs.

The biggest outrage was that the Cincinnati Reds were excluded from the postseason. Not only did they have the best record in their division — they had the best record in all of baseball. But the Los Angeles Dodgers edged them by half a game in the first half, and the Astros by a game and a half in the second half.

Who was the last umpire to use an external chest protector when working behind the plate?

Nowadays umpires working home plate are required to wear a chest protector that fits under their uniforms, but for much of the 20th century the sported an external protector known as the "bubble" — a large cushion protector that they would hold in front of their bodies like a shield. National League umpires were the first to get rid of the clunky protector, and the American League followed suit in 1977.

But like many changes in sports, the outside chest protector was grandfathered out of existence. Umpires who were active at the time of the rule change were permitted to continue using the bubble for the remainder of their careers. The last umpire to use the bubble in a game was Jerry Neudecker, who retired in 1985.

Who were the Colorado Silver Bullets?

The Colorado Silver Bullets were not notable because they were sponsored by Coors Brewery. Nor were they notable because they were an all-female team. What was notable about the Silver Bullets is that they were an all-female team playing against male competition.

At first they planned to play primarily against teams from the independent Northern League, but after being shellacked in their first games in 1994, they set more modest goals, and began playing against semi-pro and amateur teams. They finished the year 6–37.

By their fourth year, 1997, the Silver Bullets had managed a winning record, 23–22, but by then the novelty of a barnstorming team of female players had worn off, and attendance had declined. Coors pulled out as a sponsor, and the team was disbanded.

Who won 20 games in his first year in the majors, but failed to bring home Rookie of the Year honours?

Tom Browning's 1985 season was one that even a veteran would take pride in. He boasted a 20–9 record with a 3.55 ERA for the Cincinnati Reds. But this was a time when the stolen base was prized, perhaps more than at any other time in baseball history, and Vince Coleman's 110 thefts captured the hearts of voters, despite his mediocre bat. It helped that he was playing for a playoff-bound team, the St. Louis Cardinals. Coleman went on to steal more than 100 bases two more times, though he never blossomed to any great extent at the plate. Browning had some solid years, but only approached the 20-win mark once, winning 18 games in 1988.

Who managed for 27 years, winning 1,902 games, but never reached the World Series?

Sometimes you can keep on winning without winning it all. Gene Mauch had a successful career managing some outstanding ball clubs. In a career that spanned the years from 1960 to 1987, he skippered the Philadelphia Phillies, Montreal Expos, Minnesota Twins, and California Angels, capturing division titles in 1982 and 1986, both times with the Angels. Sadly, his teams were unable to win in the playoffs, and Mauch never appeared in a World Series as manager.

He did come close. In 1986, the Angels were one strike away from winning the American League Championship Series in five games, but reliever Donny Moore gave up a home run to Boston's Dave Henderson; the Sox went on to win that game, and the next two games after that. Mauch lasted only one more season as a manager.

Who was the first team to sport an identifying logo?

Merchandising was not a consideration for early baseball teams. The purpose of uniforms was to distinguish one team from another. And so, logos served little purpose.

The first team to incorporate a logo into their uniforms were the Detroit Tigers, who stitched a small, red tiger on their caps in 1901.

How many women played in the Negro Leagues?

The Negro Leagues not only provided an opportunity for black men to play baseball at a professional level, it also provided an opportunity for three women to play with the men.

Toni Stone was the first of these. She made her professional debut in 1949 with the San Francisco Sea Lions. She went on to play for the New Orleans Black Pelicans and the Indianapolis Clowns, finishing her career with the Kansas City Monarchs in 1954. Stone had a female teammate on the Indianapolis squad — Marnie "Peanut" Jackson pitched for the Clowns from 1953 to 1955, going 33–8. Finally, Connie Morgan played for the Clowns, replacing Stone after she left the team.

Ironically, though they played in a league that existed because racial intolerance would not allow black players in the major leagues, the women faced discrimination because of their gender. Toni Stone may have had the worst experience — she received almost no playing time after moving from the Clowns to the Monarchs, and was hated by her teammates.

What was the name of the professional baseball league for women that began play during World War II?

In 1943, Philip K. Wrigley founded a professional league for women. The goal of the league was to maintain a profile for baseball during the war years, when many of the top male stars were overseas and public attention was drifting away.

For convenience and clarity, the women's league is generally referred to as the All-American Girls Professional Baseball League, but it actually went by several names during its history. Between the founding of the league in 1943 and its demise after the 1954 season, it went by the names All-American Girls Professional Softball League, All-American Girls Baseball League, All-American Girls Professional Baseball League, and American Girls' Baseball League.

Was the All-American Girls Professional Baseball League actually a softball league?

The women's baseball league actually began its existence playing a game that more closely resembled softball. The original ball was 12 inches in diameter, and the pitchers threw underhanded from a mound only 40 feet from home plate. Bases were 65 feet apart.

The ball became smaller over the years, shrinking five times between 1944 and 1954. The distance between base paths was lengthened several times, topping out at 85 feet in 1954. Pitchers were still required to throw underhand, or, by 1946, sidearm, but overhand pitching was not permitted until 1948. Even then, the mound was only 50 feet from home plate and would not move to 60 feet until the last year of the league's existence.

Who competed in the first known organized game of baseball?

The first team to play using modern rules were the New York Knickerbockers, who played by what was known as the Knickerbocker Rules (developed by their founder, Alexander Cartwright). The first organized game was played between the Knickerbockers and a team known as the New York Nine. Despite inventing the rules for the game, the Knickerbockers were trounced, 23–1, in a game played at Elysian Fields in Hoboken, New Jersey.

Who is known as "The Father of Baseball"?

While it's impossible to credit any individual with inventing baseball, many are comfortable with saying the *modern* game of baseball was invented by The Father of Baseball, Alexander Cartwright. Cartwright took what was, until then, a crude stick-and-ball game and established rules that created a game that would look familiar to fans of the sport that is played today. He set the distance between bases at 90 feet, established that each team should have nine players, and forbade the former method of getting runners out by throwing the ball at them.

Besides the New York Yankees, what franchise has won the most American League pennants?

The New York Yankees have won an astonishing 40 American League Championships in their history. To put it in context, you could add together the number of pennants won by any *three* other American League teams and still not come up with a number that beats the Yankees' total.

The nearest competitor to the Yankees is the Athletics franchise, which has divided pennants between two cities: Philadelphia and Oakland. (The team also played in Kansas City, but had no first-place finishes there.)

If we limit our search to the number of pennants won in one city, the Boston Red Sox top the list with 12 American League flags.

What is "the Buckner Ball" and where is it today?

The ball that went between the legs of Bill Buckner in Game 6 of the 1986 World Series, crushing the dreams of Red Sox fans, was subsequently named The Buckner Ball. The ball was put on auction in 1992 and went to actor Charlie Sheen for $93,500. Sheen later put the ball on auction in 2000, and songwriter Seth Swirsky was the top bidder, though Swirsky refers to it as "the Mookie Ball" (the groundball that Buckner misplayed was hit by Mookie Wilson). Sheen lost money on his investment, as the ball only sold for $63,500.

Was the 1919 World Series the first to be fixed?

Though suspicions were never proven, there was plenty of speculation that three World Series were thrown prior to the famous Black Sox Scandal of 1919.

The first suspected tanking of a series took place in 1914. The heavily favoured Philadelphia Athletics were inexplicably swept in four games by the Boston Braves. Conspiracy theorists believe that the players were angry with owner Connie Mack, who paid them poorly, and decided to let the Braves win the series.

In 1917, many pointed fingers of suspicion at Heine Zimmerman, third baseman for the New York Giants, who held onto the ball during a rundown, allowing the series-winning run to score. (Zimmerman may have been unfairly accused, as there was no one to throw the ball to, but he was later implicated in another gambling scandal.) And then, in 1918, rumours were swirling that the Chicago Cubs had intentionally thrown the World Series against the Boston Red Sox.

stadiums

What does the sign "No Pepper" mean at a baseball park?

The sign "No Pepper" is seen in many baseball dugouts and refers to a game played to warm up the players. During pepper, one player bunts grounders and hits line drives to a group of infielders standing about 20 feet away. The fielders play the ball then throw it back to the batter as quickly as possible, and he then attempts to hit those return throws. Pepper is banned when spectators are in the park for fear of injury.

They Said It ...
"He was a good umpire, if you didn't tell him so too often."
Johnny Evers on Hank O'Day.

Why is the warm-up area for baseball pitchers called a "bullpen"?

As early as 1809, the term *bullpen* referred to a stockade for holding criminals. In the 1870s, a roped-off area in the outfield for standing room was nicknamed the bullpen by the *Cincinnati Enquirer*. When relief pitchers were introduced into the game they took over that area to warm up, and in a stroke of brilliance the Bull Durham Tobacco Company erected a sign overhead to confirm it as the bullpen.

Why are extra seats in a gymnasium or open-air benches in a stadium called "bleachers"?

Bleachers were used in a pinch as uncovered overflow seating from the grandstand before they became common at baseball and football games. The first recorded printed reference was in the *Chicago Tribune* on May 6, 1889. They were called "bleachers" because of their exposure to the sun. The folding seating at an inside gymnasium simply took its name from the open seating outside.

Which team attempted to become the first team to play out of a domed stadium in the 1950s?

In the 1950s, the Brooklyn Dodgers were still playing out of the beloved, but aging, Ebbett's Field. Owner Walter O'Malley was keen on building a new park for his team and contacted R. Buckminster Fuller seeking design ideas. O'Malley told Fuller that he was not just interested in building any old stadium — he wanted the Dodgers to be the first team to play out of a domed stadium.

Fuller put his graduate students on the case and came up with the design for a geodesic dome and stadium suitable for baseball.

In the meantime, O'Malley's attempts to work with the city to secure land in a prime location hit roadblock after roadblock, and the owner chose to move his team to Los Angeles. Baseball would not move indoors until the Houston Astrodome was opened in 1965.

What was the first retractable dome stadium?

When Montreal's Olympic Stadium was first built, the plan was for it to have a retractable roof operated from an inclined tower. Labour disruptions and design problems prevented the roof from being ready in time for the 1976 Olympics, or for the building's use as the home of the Montreal Expos.

When the city of Toronto began building the retractable SkyDome (now known as the Rogers Centre) for the Blue Jays, Montreal pushed to finally get their retractable roof in place before their Canadian rivals, and in 1988 Olympic Stadium became the first retractable-dome stadium in the majors; the SkyDome followed a year later.

The convertible era in Montreal was short-lived, however. The roof was difficult to operate, prone to ripping, and unsuited for use in high winds. After three seasons the roof was permanently affixed.

Players with More Than 3,000 Career Hits, and a Sub-.300 Batting Average
- Carl Yastrzemski
- Eddie Murray
- Cal Ripken
- Robin Yount
- Dave Winfield
- Craig Biggio
- Rickey Henderson
- Lou Brock
- Rafael Palmeiro
- Al Kaline

How high was Fenway Park's left field wall when originally constructed?

The Green Monster at Fenway stands at 37 feet, two inches, but it was not originally that high — nor was it green.

When Fenway first opened in 1912, its left field wall was a mere 25 feet high and was covered in advertisements. And while the high wall was a prominent feature of the park, it was not the quirkiest element. In front of the wall was a steep incline that rose 10 feet from its base in left field to its peak at the wall. The hill came to be known as Duffy's Cliff, named for left fielder Duffy Lewis, who was a master at playing balls off the slope.

Duffy's Cliff was flattened in 1934, and the wall ultimately reached its current height. But while it was a monster, it didn't turn green until 1947.

What was the first major league stadium to sell its naming rights to an outside corporation?

Traditionalists have been bemoaning the trend to sell naming rights to stadiums since the mid-1990s, though some would argue that the "trend" is actually quite old. Though Wrigley Field was named after a person rather than a brand of chewing gum, it's hard not to connect the two, given that the stadium's owner also owned the gum company.

Baseball was, nevertheless, opposed to corporate name-plugging for many years, and in 1953 rejected a proposal by Cardinals' owner Anheuser-Busch to rename St. Louis's Sportsman's Park "Budweiser Stadium." Eventually, they agreed to simply name the stadium (and its successors) Busch Stadium.

But by 1995, Major League Baseball had warmed up to the notion of corporate money, and put up no fight when the naming rights to the new home of the Colorado Rockies were sold to Coors Brewing Company, and Coors Field became the first big league stadium to officially sell naming rights.

How many stadiums have the New York Yankees called home?

Over the course of their history, the New York Yankees — under various monikers — have used six stadiums as their home ballpark.

The Yankees began life as the Baltimore Orioles in 1901. They played out of one of many stadiums in that city that went by the name "Oriole Park." After two seasons, the team moved to New York and set up shop in the newly built Hilltop Park, which had a capacity of 16,000. The team was known as the Highlanders.

In 1911 the park played host to not only the Highlanders, but the New York Giants, who were left homeless after the latest incarnation of the Polo Grounds had burnt down. Two seasons later, a new Polo Grounds opened, and both teams moved to the new facility. At the same time, the Highlanders changed their name to the Yankees.

Then, in 1923, the massive Yankee Stadium opened and New York's American League entry once again had a home park to themselves. The Yankees played there until 1973, and then made a temporary move to the Mets' Shea Stadium while Yankee Stadium underwent a massive overhaul. The Yankees returned to their old park in 1976.

Finally, a new Yankee Stadium — a near-replica of the old park — opened in 2009.

Was polo ever actually played at the Polo Grounds?

One of the early great stadiums in baseball was the Polo Grounds, which was home to the New York Giants, the New York Yankees, and the New York Mets.

The Polo Grounds that most fans are familiar with was actually the fourth stadium to bear that name. The original, built in 1876, was indeed used for polo, but became a full-time baseball stadium in 1880. That stadium was only in use until 1885. The name, however was retained, and used for three subsequent big-league stadiums.

And yet, after the original stadium, none of the subsequent Polo Grounds were ever used for polo.

What stadium did the Boston Red Sox play out of in the 1915 World Series?

Although Fenway Park had been open since 1912, the stadium could only hold about 27,000 fans. For key games such as World Series games, the Sox moved to the much larger Braves Field — home of the National League's Boston Braves. And so, in the 1915 World Series, Fenway Park remained silent as Game 3 and Game 4 were played across town.

They Said It ...
"The loss of the A's is more than recompensed by the pleasure of getting rid of Mr. Finley."
Missouri senator Stuart Symington on the move of the Kansas City Athletics — and owner Charles O. Finley — to Oakland.

Who was the first team to switch from natural grass to artificial turf?

The Astrodome in Houston was a marvel at the time — the first indoor ballpark. It was considered state of the art. One of the novel features was the use of a special grass modified for indoor use. But even this special grass required sunlight, and so transparent glass panels were included in the ceiling design.

Unfortunately, the glare of sunlight through the panels blinded fielders trying to catch fly balls, and some of the panels needed to be painted over. The grass died. In the stadium's first season, games were played on dead grass and dirt that had been painted green.

Faced with the likelihood of playing the 1966 season on a dirt field, the team looked for another solution. A company had just invented an artificial grass called ChemGrass. The Astros ordered the new turf for their second season in the Astrodome. At first, there was only enough of the plastic surface to cover the infield, but midway through the season outfield turf was installed.

To capitalize on the new venture, the makers of ChemGrass changed the name of their product to AstroTurf.

Which player demanded that the Detroit Tigers move the fences of their stadium in so that he could hit more home runs?

In 2000, two-time American League MVP Juan Gonzalez was traded to the Detroit Tigers, who were moving into the newly built Comerica Park. But as a home run hitter, Gonzalez found the new park to be a challenge — the outfield dimensions were massive. Left centre field was a whopping 395 feet from home plate.

Gonzalez struggled, hitting only 22 home runs that season, which was a huge drop considering that prior to joining the Tigers, the fewest number of home runs he'd hit was 39 home runs in each of his past four seasons.

Gonzalez, who was slated to become a free agent, demanded that the Tigers move the fences in. The Tigers refused, and Gonzalez bolted to the Cleveland Indians in 2001.

Criticism continued to plague the outfield dimensions at Comerica, and the Tigers moved the fences in for the 2003 season. By that point, even had Gonzalez still been a Tiger, injuries had taken a toll, and Gonzalez was a shadow of his former self.

> **Quickies**
> *Did you know ...*
> • that the original Wrigley Field was in Los Angeles, California? Though the Chicago stadium was built earlier, it went by the name Cubs Park. Owner William Wrigley Jr. owned both the Cubs and the minor league Los Angeles Angels, and built the L.A. Wrigley Field in 1925. The Chicago venue wasn't named Wrigley Field until 1926.

What stadium has a ladder that is in play?

Fenway Park has many quirks, not the least of which is the Green Monster in left field. The fabled wall is notable not only for its height (and for the short distance between the wall and home plate) but for the difficulties it poses for outfielders who have to judge how the ball will bounce off different parts of the wall.

A strange feature of the wall is a ladder that is attached to the wall in play. Prior to the addition of seats on top of the wall, home runs hit over the Monster landed in netting. Stadium employees would use the ladder to climb up to the top of the wall and retrieve balls from the netting.

When seats were added there was no need for ball retrieval, but the ladder remains as an essential part of the character of the ballpark.

What stadium, currently used by a major league team, was originally constructed for a team in a league that no longer exists?

It's hard to imagine Wrigley Field without the Chicago Cubs, but when the iconic stadium first opened in 1914, the Cubs were not the tenants. The stadium, then known as Weeghman Park, was built to house the Chicago Federals, the Windy City's entry in the upstart Federal League.

The Federal League was the last major challenge to the American and National Leagues, and made a valiant attempt to recruit big-name players and establish itself as a third major league. The league was a flop, and shut down after only two seasons. (In 1968 it was retroactively recognized as a major league.)

Weeghman Park was left empty, but not for long. The Federals' owner, Charlie Weeghman, teamed up with William Wrigley Jr. to purchase the Chicago Cubs and move them into the young ballpark. In the following years, Wrigley became sole owner of the team. In 1920, the park's name was changed to Cubs Park; in 1926, Wrigley threw humility aside and named the stadium after himself.

They Said It ...
"Now it is done, now the story ends. And there is no way to tell it. The art of fiction is dead. Reality has strangled invention. Only the utterly impossible, the inexpressibly fantastic, can ever be plausible again."
Sportswriter Red Smith on Bobby Thomson's 1951 pennant-winning home run.

What kind of ivy is used at Wrigley Field?

Built in 1914, Wrigley Field originally had an uncovered brick wall in the outfield that was a danger to outfielders. In 1937, Bill Veeck planted ivy plants along the wall. The ivy has grown thick over the years, and often balls get stuck in the foliage, but the frustration an outfielder might face in searching for a lost ball is a small price to pay for the safety that is provided.

The ivy of choice is Boston ivy, which is capable of surviving the harsh Chicago winters.

What was the first baseball stadium built of concrete and steel?

Concrete and steel stadiums are the norm in professional baseball, and have been for generations, but there was a time in the early years of the major leagues when all stadiums were constructed of wood. This began to change in 1909 when Shibe Park opened in Philadelphia.

Shibe Park was built for the Philadelphia Athletics at a cost of $457,167.71, and originally seated 20,000 fans. In 1925, an upper deck and outfield seats were added to bring capacity to 33,000.

The Athletics eventually moved to Kansas City and later Oakland, but Shibe Park continued to be used by the National League's Philadelphia Phillies until 1970. It was demolished in 1976.

Why did the Boston Red Sox rearrange the order of the plaques for retired numbers on their outfield wall in the 1990s?

Currently there are eight retired numbers on the wall at Fenway Park, but for many years, the numbers of Ted Williams (9), Joe Cronin (4), Bobby Doerr (1), and Carl Yastrzemski (8) were the only numbers on display, and they were arranged in that order.

In the 1980s, media began fabricating the "Curse of the Bambino." The supposed "curse" was a hex Babe Ruth placed on the team after being sold to the Yankees. Ruth never actually placed any curse on the team, but it made for a nice story. In 1989, a new piece was added to the myth when Yastrzemski's number was retired. Someone observed that the order of the numbers, if seen as a date, would be 9–4–18 — September 4, 1918. That date was the night before the 1918 World Series — the last that the Red Sox had won. As much of a stretch as it was, this was useful information to curse theorists.

In the 1990s, the numbers were arranged in order — 1, 4, 8, 9 — in an effort to break the curse. The rewards were not immediate, but curse believers will tell you that if the numbers had not been re-ordered, the Red Sox would not have won the World Series in 2004 and 2007.

What happened to the lights that were supposed to be installed in Wrigley Field in 1941?

Wrigley Field was long known as the last hold out against night baseball, playing 5,687 consecutive day games before lights were finally installed and night games played in 1988.

But the holdout was almost a brief one. In 1941, lights were delivered to Wrigley Field for the purpose of lighting the stadium for night games for the 1942 season. But the day after the Japanese bombed Pearl Harbor, a patriotic William Wrigley donated the lights to a shipyard to aid in the war effort.

As time went on, day games became a nearly unbreakable tradition. But by the late 1980s, the lack of lights became an issue, to the point that Major League Baseball was threatening to force the Cubs to play postseason games at Busch Stadium in St. Louis — an unthinkable penalty for Cards-hating Cubs fans. So, on August 8, the Cubs started their first night game at Wrigley.

The baseball gods must have been reluctant to part with tradition; the game was called due to rain after three innings, and the official night game at Wrigley wasn't played until the following evening.

What is the only monument in Yankee Stadium's Monument Park that is not dedicated to a specific person?

One of the most famous features of the old and new Yankee Stadiums is Monument Park. Once located on the playing field before being moved behind the outfield wall in the 1970s, the section of the park honours former Yankee greats with plaques and monuments.

But one plaque is not dedicated to an individual — it is dedicated to a group of people. On September 11, 2002, one year after the attacks on the World Trade Center, a plaque was placed in the back right corner of Monument Park in honour of the victims and rescue workers of 9/11.

What was the "Black Monster"?

For two years, in 2001 and 2002, part of the outfield at Cincinnati's Cinergy Field (formerly Riverfront Stadium) was demolished to make room for The Great American Ballpark, which was being built immediately next to Cinergy. But despite the partial demolition, Cinergy Field was still used for Reds games.

The removal of outfield seats created a less than ideal backdrop for hitters, so a 40-foot black wall was erected in center field. The wall was in play, and for two seasons the wall, known as the Black Monster, was the highest outfield wall in the Majors.

The Reds moved to their new stadium and Cinergy was completely levelled.

What stadium has a section called the "Uecker seats"?

Bob Uecker was a mediocre ballplayer (his lifetime batting average was an even .200), but he became known as "Mr. Baseball" after his playing career thanks to his antics as a broadcaster, actor, and pitchman.

Uecker appeared in a series of beer commercials for Miller Lite. In one of the most memorable, Uecker is attending a baseball game when an usher tells him he's in the wrong seat. Uecker follows the usher, saying "I must be in the front row!" He's then escorted to upper deck seats behind a post.

Thereafter, fans and media began referring to seats far from the action, or with obstructed views, as "Uecker seats." It was Milwaukee's

Miller Park that officially gave the name to a section of the stands. Seats in that section are blocked by the pivot for the stadium roof. On the bright side, the tickets only cost one dollar.

What is the highest outfield wall in professional baseball?

While Fenway's Green Monster is without doubt the most famous outfield wall in the sport, it's not the highest. That honour goes to the Arch Nemesis, the left field wall at Sovereign Bank Stadium in York, Pennsylvania. The park is the home of the York Revolution of the independent Atlantic League of Professional Baseball.

Sovereign Bank Stadium opened its doors for the 2007 stadium, with the Arch Nemesis measuring 37 feet, eight inches — a mere six inches higher than the Green Monster at Fenway Park.

When was the first World Series played entirely on artificial turf?

The World Series had been played on AstroTurf twice before — in 1975 and 1976 — but only one team (the Cincinnati Reds in both series) played in a stadium with an artificial surface. It wasn't until 1980 that a World Series was played entirely on artificial grass. That year, the Philadelphia Phillies defeated the Kansas City Royals, four games to two. Philadelphia had been playing on AstroTurf at Veterans' Stadium since 1971, and the Royals had been playing on the plastic since Royals Stadium (now Kauffman Stadium) was built in 1973.

Royals Stadium was the only stadium built as a baseball-only facility to use artificial grass. In 1995, as teams around the Majors were moving to more traditional stadiums, real grass was installed, ending the plastic era in Kansas City.

fact or fiction?

Did Babe Ruth call his home run in the 1932 World Series?

Babe Ruth and the New York Yankees rolled into Chicago for Game 3 of the 1932 World Series with a 2–0 series lead. The Babe felt the wrath of Cubs fans upon arrival — and so did his wife. The two were booed in a local restaurant. At the stadium for Game 3, Ruth was heckled mercilessly, particularly after he dropped a fly ball that allowed the tying run to score.

In the fifth inning, Ruth stepped to the plate against Charley Root. According to the legend, Ruth then raised his arm and pointed to centre field, vowing to hit a home run into the centre field bleachers. On the next pitch, he did just that.

Did it really happen? In all likelihood, no. Players on both teams have said Ruth never called his shot, and was merely taunting the Cubs bench by pointing out how many strikes he had (and presumably indicating that he wasn't bothered). Even Ruth denied that he called his shot for years, though later in life he was willing to let the legend thrive.

So, it makes for a good story, and some fun action in the otherwise terrible movies that have been made about Ruth's life, but the story is fictional.

Did the seventh-inning stretch begin when U.S. President William Howard Taft stood during a game?

As the story goes, President Taft was attending an opening-day matchup between the Washington Senators and the Philadelphia Athletics on April 14, 1910. In the middle of the seventh inning, Taft stood up to stretch his legs. The other fans in attendance thought that he was getting up to leave and, as was customary, they stood as well to show their respect to the departing head of state. But Taft didn't leave, and he and the spectators remained standing until play resumed. Thus began the tradition of the seventh-inning stretch.

Or so we're told.

Whether Taft ever took the opportunity to stretch his legs at a game or not, the tradition predates Taft's presidency by many years. As far back as 1869, Harry Wright, a player with the Cincinatti Red Stockings, described in a letter a Cincinatti custom of standing during the seventh-inning break.

Does a corked bat make a ball travel further?

After Sammy Sosa was famously caught using a corked bat after it shattered on impact, there was plenty of debate over whether a corked bat actually helps the ball to travel further. It is now commonly felt that a corked bat has negligible impact on a ball, or if anything, it actually hinders the ball's flight.

Many studies would seem to back this, including an episode of *MythBusters*, which appeared to demonstrate that a ball travels a significantly shorter distance off a corked bat.

But other studies contradict this. Most notable, as a study by the University of Massachusetts Baseball Research Center in 2003 demonstrated, was that a corked bat swung at the same speed as a solid bat created a spring effect that actually increased the speed of the ball after impact by 2 percent. It's a small difference, but would add anywhere from five to 10 feet of distance to a ball hit to the warning track.

The University of Massachusetts study is considered one of the most carefully executed studies of bat doctoring.

Players with More Than 2,000 Career Runs Scored	
Player	Career Runs
Rickey Henderson	2,295
Ty Cobb	2,246
Barry Bonds	2,227
Hank Aaron	2,174
Babe Ruth	2,174
Pete Rose	2,165
Willie Mays	2,062

Was the World Series named after the *New York World* newspaper?

Over the years, a common belief has developed that says the World Series took its name from the contest's original sponsor, the now-defunct *New York World* newspaper.

However, the story is baseless. The *World* was never involved in the World Series in any way, except to cover the games. They were not a sponsor, and had no affiliation with the games. What's more, the term *World Series* wasn't even universally adopted at that time. The series was known by several descriptive names, such as the World Series, the World's Series, and the World Championship Series.

In the early 2000s, a researcher from the Hall of Fame tried to authenticate the urban legend, but found that it had no basis in fact.

Was Babe Ruth sold to the Yankees to finance the production of the musical *No, No, Nanette*?

Strictly speaking, no. But there is some element of truth in the story, which keeps it out of "urban legend" territory.

Harry Frazee, owner of the Boston Red Sox, made one of the most famous blunders in baseball history when he sold Babe Ruth to the New York Yankees in 1917. The Yankees went on to become the most winning franchise in baseball history, while the Red Sox — until that point a dominant force in the game — would not win a World Series again for another 87 years.

Years later, it was said that Ruth was sold to the Yankees so that Frazee, a theatre producer, could finance the musical *No, No, Nanette*. In fact, *No, No, Nanette* was not even produced for another five years.

However, the money earned from the sale of Babe Ruth did help to finance another Frazee play, *My Lady Friends*. A non-musical, the play had a run on Broadway. A few years later, a musical version of *My Lady Friends* was produced: *No, No, Nanette*.

So, while *No, No Nanette* was not financed by the sale of Ruth, it likely would not have seen the light of day if not for the trade. Presumably, Red Sox fans do not see this as a silver lining.

They Said It ...
"It scares me. Scares the hell out of me. You have no idea where you're going to throw the ball. You're afraid you might hurt someone." *Pitcher Steve Blass on the mental block that caused him to make wild pitches.*

When did Major League Baseball remove the asterisk from Roger Maris's home run record in the official record books?

Baseball never removed the asterisk from Maris's home run record, because the asterisk never existed in the first place.

When Roger Maris was approaching Babe Ruth's single-season home run record (60) in 1961, commissioner Ford Frick — who had been a close friend of Ruth's before Ruth passed — announced that, since Ruth hit his 60 home runs in a 154-game season and Maris was headed toward breaking that record in a 162-game season, the two records should be listed separately, meaning that Maris's would be the lesser record.

However, Major League Baseball didn't actually keep official lists of records such as the home run record. Record books were compiled by independent writers, editors, and publishers. If they were to put an asterisk next to Maris's record, they would be doing so by choice, but "officially," there was no record to place an asterisk next to.

Did Fidel Castro try out for the New York Yankees?

Imagine how the latter half of the 20th century would have been different if Fidel Castro had been signed by the New York Yankees when he tried out for them during the days before he got a hankering for revolution.

Or, imagine that there was even a grain of truth to this urban legend.

Despite the popularity of different versions of the story, Fidel Castro never tried out for the New York Yankees, Washington Senators, or any other U.S. baseball team.

It is true that American scouts had seen Castro pitch — the Pittsburgh Pirates were one of many major league teams scouting in Cuba during the pre-revolutionary era, and one of their talent-seekers had watched Castro in Havana. But while Castro had a decent curveball, the scout didn't think he had enough zip on his fastball to make it in the U.S.

Who first used "Holy Cow" as a signature call, Harry Caray or Phil Rizzuto?

Harry Caray, best known as a long-time Cubs and Cardinals broadcaster, and Phil Rizzuto, a Hall of Fame Yankees shortstop and, later, broadcaster, both made liberal use of the phrase "Holy Cow" when working in the booth.

While Rizzuto did not use the phrase to imitate Caray — he had been saying "Holy Cow" since his youth to avoid swearing — Caray was the first of the two to use the words when calling a game, and had established them as his signature call before Rizzuto ever stepped into the booth.

Why was Abner Doubleday credited with inventing baseball?

According to legend, in the summer of 1839, Abner Doubleday, who was enrolled at the United States Military Academy en route to a career in the military, took time out from his busy life to invent the game of baseball in a farmer's field in Cooperstown, New York.

That, at least, was the finding of a National League committee set up to determine the origins of the game in 1907. In reality, the only thing Abner Doubleday started was the Civil War (he fired the first shot for the North at Fort Sumter when the Union and the Confederacy turned words into action in 1861).

The committee's findings were almost pure fiction, and it seemed to many observers that their goal was merely to establish that baseball was invented in the United States, and when that failed, they turned to mythmaking. The best piece of evidence they could come up with for the Doubleday theory was the testimony of a single man, Abner Graves, who produced a ball that he said Doubleday used when inventing the sport. Graves was later placed in a mental institution after murdering his wife, so it's possible that he wasn't the most credible witness in the world.

Meanwhile, in the many journals Doubleday kept, he never mentions the game of baseball and there is no record of him ever claiming to have been involved with the sport in any way.

Three Players with 20 or More Home Runs in a Season, and a Sub-.200 Batting Average			
Year	Player, Team	Batting Average	Most Home Runs in a Season
1991	Rob Deer, Detroit Tigers	.179 AVG	25 home runs
1999	Ruben Rivera, San Diego Padres	.195 AVG	23 home runs
2001	Mark McGwire, St. Louis Cardinals	.187 AVG	29 home runs

Nonetheless, a good story is a good story, and the town of Cooperstown is a Mecca for baseball fans around the world who come to visit the Hall of Fame and Doubleday field, where the mythical first game was played.

Did the Yankees start wearing pinstripes to make Babe Ruth look slimmer?

The New York Yankees uniforms are often referred to simply as "the Pinstripes." It has been said that they first started wearing pinstripes after acquiring Babe Ruth. Pinstripes are said to make a person look slimmer, and Ruth was a man who could stand to lose a few pounds.

Like a lot of baseball lore, this is pure myth. The New York team had been wearing pinstripes as far back as 1912, when they were known as the New York Highlanders.

So, while pinstripes may have helped to make Ruth look slimmer, that wasn't the reason the Yankees started wearing them.

Has a player ever played in a Major League Baseball game and a National Football League game on the same day?

In the 1990s Deion Sanders managed to play both football and baseball professionally, but was confronted with the same problem every season: the end of the Major League Baseball season overlaps with the beginning of the NFL season. In 1992, Sanders was a member of both the Atlanta Braves and the Atlanta Falcons. The Braves were headed for the playoffs, and Sanders elected to stick with his baseball team. The Falcons fined him $68,000 for missing the first games of the season. So, in a desire to appease his football team and make history at the same time, Sanders attempted to play two games on one day.

It would have been easier had both teams been playing in Atlanta that day. Instead, he travelled to Miami for an afternoon game between the Falcons and Dolphins, then flew to Pittsburgh for a National League Championship Series game between the Braves and Pirates in the evening.

Urban legend has it that Sanders played in both games that day. Unfortunately for the legend, and for Deion, Braves manager Bobby Cox did not play Sanders that night.

They Said It ...
"It would have been a hell of a lot more fun if I had not hit those 61 home runs."
Roger Maris.

Did a boy really ask Shoeless Joe Jackson to "Say it ain't so"?

In 1920, as he and his Chicago White Sox teammates stood trial for throwing the 1919 World Series, Shoeless Joe Jackson admitted to receiving payments from gamblers, though he maintained that he did not himself do anything to cause his team to lose games.

According to a published news report, as Joe left the courthouse a young boy grabbed Jackson's sleeve and said, "It ain't true, is it, Joe?" to which Jackson replied, "Yes, kid, I'm afraid it is." It has been suggested that the report was a fabrication designed to show the innocence that the Black Sox had shattered. Jackson himself, in a 1949 article, said that the conversation never occurred.

At the very least, the famous wording, "Say it ain't so, Joe," is a myth, and there's a good chance that the boy himself was a fictional construct.

Did Ty Cobb really beat up a handicapped fan?

Ty Cobb was a jerk — that much everyone could agree on. He was surly, and often slid into bases spikes-up in an attempt to break up plays, even if it meant injuring his opponents. But his most notorious act is also one that has been twisted various ways for nearly a century.

All versions of the story are clear on two points: 1) Ty Cobb physically attacked a heckler in the stands, and 2) that said heckler was handicapped. Both points are true, but the second point has been interpreted in different ways. Some stories have the "handicap" as being paralysis, some have it as missing arms, and some claim that the assault victim had no limbs whatsoever.

In truth, the man, Claude Lueker, had been injured in a printing press accident. He was missing and three fingers on the one hand and the other hand altogether.

When did people start referring to the "Curse of the Bambino"?

The "Curse of the Bambino" refers to an apparent curse that Babe Ruth placed on the Boston Red Sox when they sold him to the New York Yankees in 1920. It is said that Ruth hexed the Sox so that they would never win another World Series.

If Ruth did place such a hex on the Sox, nobody learned of the curse for more than 65 years. It wasn't until the mid-1980s — and specifically, after the infamous Game 6 collapse in the 1986 World Series — that anyone made reference to any Curse of the Bambino.

Was the Baby Ruth candy bar named after Babe Ruth?

> **They Said It ...**
> Interviewer: "We're going to play free association. I'm going to mention a name, and Yogi's just going to say the first thing that comes to mind. Okay, Yogi?"
> Yogi Berra: "Okay."
> Interviewer: "All right, here we go then. Mickey Mantle."
> Yogi Berra: "What about him?"

The Curtiss Candy Company introduced the Baby Ruth candy bar in 1921. Since that time, they have claimed that the introduction of Baby Ruth at a time that slugger Babe Ruth was capturing the hearts of millions was merely a coincidence. According to Curtiss, the bar was named after Ruth Cleveland, the daughter of former U.S. president Grover Cleveland.

Ruth, they say, toured the company's facilities years earlier when they were starting out, and her visit touched the company owner to the point that he decided to name a candy bar after her.

The company's claims are suspect. First, Ruth died in 1904, 12 years before the Curtiss Candy Company was founded. Visiting the company's facilities would have been quite a feat (though it would certainly have been memorable). Second, the story doesn't explain why someone old enough to tour the factory would be called "Baby Ruth."

Curtiss also claims that Babe Ruth wasn't well known at the time the bar was introduced. In fact, Ruth had already begun playing for the New York Yankees. He'd already shattered his own home run record by slugging 54 home runs in 1920, and 59 in 1921. He was one of the most famous men on the planet.

rules and lingo

Why is an erratic person called a "screwball"?

In baseball, when a pitcher throws a curveball it breaks to a right-hander's left and a left-hander's right. Early in the 20th century, the great Christy Mathewson came up with a pitch that broke in the opposite direction and completely baffled opposing batters, who called it a "screwball." It became a word used to describe anything eccentric or totally surprising — including the behaviour of human "screwballs."

What is a "corked bat"?

Some baseball players (like Sammy Sosa) believe that the spring from a "corked bat" adds distance to a struck ball and even though physicists say this is nonsense, occasionally someone will try to use one. The basic method of corking a bat is to drill a straight hole into the top, about one inch wide and 10 inches deep. Then, after filling it with cork, plug the hole with a piece of wood and sand it smooth. A corked bat is illegal only if used in play.

Why do we call a leg injury a "charley horse"?

The phrase "charley horse" has its roots in baseball. At the beginning of the 20th century, groundskeepers often used old and lame horses to pull the equipment used to keep the playing field in top condition. The Baltimore Orioles had a player named Charley Esper who, after years of injuries, walked with pain. Because his limp reminded his teammates of the groundskeeper's lame horse, they called Esper "Charley Horse."

What are the seven different ways a baseball batter can reach first base?

In baseball, a batter can reach first base with a hit, or by being walked with four balls. He also goes to first if he is struck by a pitch or if the catcher interferes with his batting. If the catcher drops the ball on strike three or the pitcher throws the ball out of the playing area the batter moves to first.

Finally, the seventh way a batter can get on base is if the baseball becomes stuck in the umpire's mask or equipment.

> **They Said It ...**
> "My favourite word in English, and I love this word, is *youneverknow*."
> *Joaquin Andujar.*

Why is the position between second base and third base called *shortstop*?

Baseball began with four outfielders and only three infielders to guard the bases. In 1849, D.L. Adams (1814–1899) realized that three men could cover fly balls in the outfield and that by moving one of these outfield players to the infield he could keep a lot of ground balls from getting through by "stopping them short," thus giving the new position its name of shortstop. Technically, this position is still an outfielder.

Why does the letter *K* signify a strikeout on a baseball score sheet?

Early in baseball history, a man named Henry Chadwick designed the system we still use for keeping score. Because his system already had an overabundance of Ss scattered throughout his score sheet — safe, slide, shortstop, sacrifice, second base, etc. — he decided to use the last letter of *struck*, as in, "he struck out," rather than the first. And that's why K signifies a strikeout in baseball.

Why do we call someone who is left-handed a "southpaw"?

When the first baseball diamonds were laid out there were no night games. To keep the afternoon or setting sun out of the batters' eyes, home plate was positioned so that the hitter was facing east, which meant the pitcher was facing west. Most pitchers threw with their right arm, but the rare and dreaded left-hander's pitching arm was on the more unfamiliar south side, and he was referred to, with respect, as a southpaw.

How did *rhubarb* become baseball slang for a fight or argument?

Legendary Brooklyn Dodgers broadcaster Red Barber first used *rhubarb* on-air to describe a baseball altercation in 1943. He said he heard it from reporter Garry Shumacher, who picked it up from another reporter, Tom Meany, who learned it from an unnamed Brooklyn bartender. The anonymous bartender used it to describe an incident in his establishment when a Brooklyn fan shot a Giants fan.

Why is someone out of touch said to be "out in left field"?

"Out in left field" means to be misguided or lost, but it generally means to be out of touch with the action. In baseball, left field is generally no more remote then centre or right field, but in Yankee Stadium, when right fielder Babe Ruth was an active player, the choice outfield seats were near the Bambino. Fans in the right field stands derided those "losers" far from the action as being out in left field.

Quickies
Did you know ...
- that Babe Ruth is the only player to have more than 2,000 hits, runs, RBIs, and walks? He had 2,873 hits, 2,174 runs, 2,217 RBIs, and 2,062 walks.

Why do we say that someone who is sharp is "on the ball"?

To be "on the ball" means to be at the top of your game. We have all heard a pitcher's excuse of not having his "stuff" after a bad outing and wondered how that excuse would work with our bosses if we had a bad day. From the early days of baseball, when a pitcher couldn't find the spin and lost control, it's been said he had "nothing on the ball" which gave us "on the ball" as meaning "he's in control."

Why do we say that someone in control has the "upper hand"?

Someone with the "upper hand" has the final say over a situation. When a group of youngsters gather to pick sides at a game of sandlot baseball, the two captains decide who chooses first when one of them grasps the bat at the bottom of the handle. The captains take turns gripping the bat one fist over the other until there was no more room. The last one to fully grip the bat handle has first choice. He has the upper hand.

> **Quickies**
> *Did you know ...*
> * that in 1885 a rule permitted baseball bats to have one flat side?

What is the advantage of "sitting in the catbird seat"?

"Sitting in the catbird seat" means you have an advantage over the opposition. The catbird is a thrush, and like its cousin, the mockingbird, perches among the highest branches of a tree and has a warning cry that resembles that of a cat. "Sitting in the catbird seat" originated in the U.S. South in the 19th century and was regularly used on radio by Red Barber (1908–1992), the Brooklyn Dodgers' baseball announcer. Amused by the expression, Dodgers fan and humorist James Thurber (1894–1961) popularized the expression in a 1942 *New Yorker* story entitled "The Catbird Seat." As Thurber wrote, "'Sitting in the catbird seat' meant sitting pretty, like a batter with three balls and no strikes on him."

Why is an easily caught pop–up called a "can of corn"?

The legend is that in the days before supermarkets, small grocery store owners placed their tins of canned corn on the top shelves because it stored well, and didn't sell as quickly as fresh corn. For most customers, this put the cans out of reach. The store owner or clerk would need a broomstick to reach up and topple the "can of corn" from the shelf and easily catch it by hand or in an apron.

Why are the pitcher and catcher collectively called the "battery"?

A "battery" is a military term for "artillery," and its use in baseball to describe a pitcher and catcher alludes to the fact that the "battery" is the principle attack force for the small army of nine players within a field contest. There is also an earlier theory that it comes from telegraphy, where the word "battery" (also borrowed from artillery) defines the sender (pitcher) and the receiver (catcher).

What is the technical name for Tommy John surgery?

The dreaded surgery that signals the end of a pitcher's season goes by the technical name, *ulnar collateral ligament reconstruction*. Mercifully, in the popular vocabulary the surgery has been named for Tommy John, the first professional athlete to undergo the elbow reconstruction.

The surgery was pioneered by Dr. Frank Jobe, and is performed when an athlete (usually a pitcher) damages his elbow ligament irreparably. A surgeon will take a ligament from another part of the athlete's body — usually the non-throwing forearm or below the knee — and insert that ligament in place of the damaged elbow ligament.

Though Tommy John surgery generally ends a pitcher's season, the success rate is over 90 percent. In fact, many pitchers not only return to form, but can actually throw harder after the surgery.

As for Tommy John — after undergoing the procedure late in the 1974 season, he returned in 1976 and continued to pitch for 14 more seasons, winning an additional 164 games.

What is the Infield Fly Rule?

Even knowledgeable baseball fans sometimes fumble over themselves trying to explain the Infield Fly Rule.

The key to understanding the rule is to remember its purpose: to prevent infielders from intentionally dropping a fly ball in order to make an easy double play against runners who have been forced to tag up.

There are two criteria that must exist for the rule to be called: 1) there have to be fewer than two outs; and 2) there must be a force at third base or at home plate. If a fly ball is hit that a fielder should be able to catch with "ordinary effort," as stated in the rule book, the batter is called out. The umpire must signal and verbalize the call so that the runners know the implications.

After the rule is called, the ball is NOT dead. The base runners are free to decide whether to attempt to advance to the next base.

Who was the last pitcher to throw a legal spitball?

The spitball was once a common feature in the arsenal of many big league hurlers, but became controversial. While the purpose of applying spit to baseballs was to affect ball flight, there was a side effect: because the spit in question was loaded with tobacco juice, balls became dark and hard to see. When batter Ray Chapman was hit in the head and killed by a spitball in 1920, many blamed the death on a hard-to-see ball.

After the 1920 season, spitballs were outlawed. However, the 17 pitchers who were currently using the spitball were allowed to continue doing so for the rest of their careers. Burleigh Grimes was the last of these pitchers to retire, in 1934.

names

Why do the White Sox and Red Sox spell their names with *X*s?

Both the Chicago White Sox and Boston Red Sox began their histories with different names entirely. The White Sox first drew breath as the Chicago Invaders. The Red Sox were known at different times as the Boston Puritans and the Boston Pilgrims.

It was the Chicago team that first decided to name themselves after clothing, and Boston followed suit. They were known, respectively, as the White Stockings and Red Stockings. Newspapers, always looking for ways to save space in headlines, shortened the team names to "Socks," then even further to "Sox." Thus began years of debate over how to properly punctuate the possessive form of the names.

Why is the L.A. baseball team called the Dodgers?

Before moving to Los Angeles, the Dodgers were based in Brooklyn, New York. The team had originated in the 19th century when, because of the dangers of horse-drawn trolleys and carriages, the pedestrians of Brooklyn called themselves "trolley dodgers." Because most of their working-class fans had to dodge traffic on their walk to the games, the Brooklyn baseball team named themselves the "Dodgers" in their honour. When the team moved to L.A. in the 1950s, they took the name with them.

Ten Great Nicknames
- Mr. October (Reggie Jackson)
- The Big Hurt (Frank Thomas)
- Donald "Duke" Snider
- Joltin' Joe DiMaggio
- Steve "Bye Bye" Balboni
- Senor Smoke (Aurelio Lopez)
- The Crime Dog (Fred McGriff)
- The Human Rain Delay (Mike Hargrove)
- The Splendid Splinter (Ted Williams)
- Louisiana Lightning (Ron Guidry)

What team was known as the Blue Jays long before a team existed in Toronto?

When R.R.M. Carpenter, the heir to the DuPont empire, purchased the Philadelphia Phillies in 1943, he turned the team over to his son, R.R.M.

Carpenter Jr. The younger Carpenter was, presumably, thrilled to be a team owner, but knew that he was taking over a team with a history of losing. So, he decided the easiest way to stop people from saying "the Phillies stink" would be to change the team's name. After a city-wide vote, the new name, "Blue Jays," was chosen.

The name change was never made official, however. The team's uniforms still said "Phillies," and the only sign of any change was a logo of a blue jay that the players wore on their sleeves. The logo was a curious one, showing a bird bent over in an act of either searching for worms or throwing up.

The new nickname never caught on, and by 1949 the logo had been dropped and the team stopped referring to itself as anything other than the Phillies. A quarter of a century later, the name was revived when, in another city-wide name-the-team contest, several fans suggested "Blue Jays" as the name for Toronto's expansion franchise.

Which team's name has been in use longer than any other team in the major leagues?

When the Worcester Brown Stockings of the National League folded, a new team, the Philadelphia Quakers, replaced them for the 1883 season. As was the custom in those days, the team was often referred to as "the Philadelphias" by fans and media. Newspapers often shortened this in headlines to "Phillies." For much of the 1880s, the team was known interchangeably as the Phillies and Quakers, but in 1890, the name "Phillies" was officially adopted. Though the team had other unofficial names over the years, "Phillies" has endured as the longest team name in continuous use in the Majors.

Where did the New York Mets get their name?

When New York was awarded a National League expansion franchise for the 1962 season, a number of names were discussed. Some were awful, such as the Bees, the Burros, and the Skyscrapers. Ownership reached into the history books and discovered that there was once a team called the New York Metropolitans in the early professional league known as the American Association. It was a strange choice, with the historical significance of the name being dubious at best. The earlier Metropolitans had modest success, but ultimately folded as they were unable to compete for fans with the city's National League team, the New York Gothams (later known as the Giants).

When the name was revived in the 1960s, initially the official name was "Metropolitans," with "Mets" used on the team uniforms. Eventually, the official team name was shortened to "Mets."

How many home runs did "Home Run" Baker hit?

Frank Baker earned the nickname "Home Run" Baker thanks to two clutch bombs in the 1911 World Series that helped his Philadelphia Athletics win the championship four games to two.

In those days of the "dead ball," home runs were more of a novelty. Two key round trippers in a single series were considered impressive. And Baker was far from a one-series wonder: he led the American League in home runs four years in a row, hitting 11 in 1911, 10 in 1912, 12 in 1913, and nine in 1914. His career total was 96. Clearly, times were different.

Baker would later join the New York Yankees, finishing his career in 1922. Though he was still approaching double-digits in home runs in his final years, his fame was dwindling. His teammate, Babe Ruth, was redefining the home run.

How "wee" was Wee Willie Keeler?

Though some sources have listed Keeler at 5'4", it's most likely that he was three inches taller than that. Still, at 5'7", Keeler is one of the shortest members of the Hall of Fame. And at a mere 140 pounds, he's also one of the lightest.

In the late 19th and early 20th century, Keeler was a star with the Brooklyn Superbas and the Baltimore Orioles team that moved to New York, later taking the name Yankees. The small outfielder wasn't much of a power threat, but was a productive singles hitter, and ranks 14th in career batting average (.341). One of his most famous skills, perfected while an Oriole, was his "Baltimore chop": he would hit the ball down into the ground so that by the time it had bounced into the air and came down in a fielder's mitt they would have no time to throw him out at first base. He once hit safely in 45 consecutive games — a record that stood until broken by Joe DiMaggio in 1941.

Who was known as "The Human Rain Delay"?

Mike Hargrove became better known as a manager, but he also had an outstanding career as a first baseman with the Texas Rangers and Cleveland Indians. Though his power numbers were modest, he was an on-base freak, with a career OBP of .396.

As good as he was as a player, his abilities were often overshadowed by his antics between pitches while batting. Hargrove had what was likely the most elaborate series of rituals the game has ever seen. Before each pitch he would make adjustments to his helmet, batting gloves, and various parts of his uniform. The routine was so lengthy that the media began referring to him as "The Human Rain Delay." Pitchers were so frustrated by the rhythm-busting routine that Hargrove eventually had to be ordered to speed things up, and later in his career the routine was considerably shorter.

How many franchises have gone by the name "Washington Senators"?

The original Washington Senators franchise was a short-lived entry in the American Association and National League from 1891 to 1899.

This franchise was mothballed when the National League contracted at the end of the century, and two years later a new Washington Senators team emerged in the American League. This team lasted from 1901 to 1960, before moving to Minneapolis and St. Paul to become the Minnesota Twins.

Washington was not without a team for long, though. Major League Baseball, afraid they would lose their coveted anti-trust exemption, awarded a new team to the city to begin play in 1961. This team lasted until 1971, and then moved to Texas.

So, three teams have existed with the name Washington Senators, though only two teams still play that once went by that name.

> **Quickies**
> *Did you know ...*
> • that Reggie Jackson, despite hitting 563 career home runs, never hit more than 30 in back-to-back seasons? He is the only player with more than 450 home runs who never topped 30 in consecutive years.

How many franchises have gone by the name "St. Louis Browns"?

Many fans know that the Baltimore Orioles originally came from St. Louis, and were known at one time as the St. Louis Browns. But they weren't the first team to bear that name, nor are they the only team in existence that was once the Browns.

The first team to go by that name actually did so unofficially. When the National League was founded in 1876, one of its charter members was the St. Louis Brown Stockings, who often went by the shortened name, the Browns. The team only lasted through the 1877 season.

Five years later, a new St. Louis Browns team emerged in the American Association. The Browns dominated the AA for several years, but when the league collapsed the team was forced to move to the National League in 1892. In 1899, they changed their name to the Perfectos, though that name only stuck for one season. Since 1900, they have been known as the Cardinals.

How did the Philadelphia/Kansas City/ Oakland Athletics get their name?

The Athletics' name dates back to the first of three Philadelphia teams to go by the name *Athletics*. The first was founded as an amateur squad in 1860, taking the name *Athletic Base Ball Club of Philadelphia* (though the "of Philadelphia" part was only used to distinguish this club from other "Athletic Base Ball Clubs" from other cities). Newspapers of the time called the team "the Athletics" as a convenient short form.

The original team turned pro in the late 1860s when they joined the National Association, then, in 1876, the National League. Financial troubles doomed the club, however.

In 1882 another edition of the Philadelphia Athletics was founded. This team lasted until 1890.

Finally, the current franchise was a charter member of the American League in 1901. They moved to Kansas City in 1955, and Oakland in 1968.

Why do the Oakland Athletics have an elephant as their mascot?

The strange choice of an elephant as the mascot for the Athletics dates back to the early 1900s when the team was based in Philadelphia. John McGraw, the colourful manager of the New York Giants, mocked the team, calling them a "white elephant." (A "white elephant" is a possession that is more expensive to maintain than it is actually worth, yet the owner is unable to get rid of it.) To thumb their noses at McGraw's slight, the team made the white elephant their mascot, and began sporting elephant logos on their sleeves.

> **They Said It ...**
> "Babe Ruth? I knew Ruth. Left-handed hitter. Hit a lot of home runs. Used to be a pitcher."
> *Edd Roush.*

How did the San Diego Padres get their name?

The major league version of the San Diego Padres took the name from a minor league team of the same name ... but how did the word *padres* become applied to baseball?

The earlier version of the team began life in 1903 as the Sacramento Solons of the Pacific Coast League. They bounced around for many years, from Sacramento, to Tacoma, back to Sacramento, then on to San Francisco, Salt Lake City, Los Angeles, and finally, San Diego. Among the team names during its travels was the San Francisco Missions, a name that paid homage to the Franciscan Missions that played a role in California history. The newly located San Diego team revisited that reference by adopting the name "Padres." This PCL team was the heart of San Diego baseball from 1936 to 1968 when owner C. Arnholt Smith was granted a National League expansion team and folded the PCL team, taking its name with him.

Why is the Cleveland team called the "Indians"?

The early Cleveland team, which was one of the original American League teams, went by several other names in its early years: the Bluebirds, the Blues, and the Bronchos. After the great second baseman Nap Lajoie joined the team, they were named the Naps in his honour, but when Lajoie was sold to the Philadelphia Athletics, a new name was in order.

After discussion with local media, ownership settled on "Indians." Urban legend has it that the team was named after Louis Sockalexis, the Native American who played for another Cleveland team in the late 1890s. However, it's more likely that the Cleveland team was simply trying to capitalize on the success of the World Champion Boston Braves by adopting a similar nickname.

Why did the Cincinnati Reds remove their team name from their jerseys for a brief period in the 1950s?

One of the uglier aspects of the 1950s was the witch hunt that came to be known as McCarthyism, when Senator Joe McCarthy led an effort to eliminate the threat of communism from the United States, going to irrational lengths along the way.

An example of the paranoia that this period evoked is the Cincinnati Reds' decision to change their name and uniforms. Though the name "Reds" had nothing to do with communism, the team was afraid of any connection, even a superficial one, being made, and in 1956 they officially changed their name to the Redlegs and removed the word *Reds* from their jerseys. The word "Reds" did not appear on team uniforms again until 1961.

Why is Kansas City's team called the Royals?

Kansas City was once home to a Negro Leagues team called the Kansas City Monarchs, a team that featured a number of the game's great players. The similarity of the names "Royals" and "Monarchs" has led many to assume that the current team took its name from the earlier squad.

In fact, the Kansas City Royals were named after the American Royal Livestock Show, an annual Kansas tradition dating back to 1899.

Why do the Los Angeles Angels have "of Anaheim" at the end of their name?

The original Angels team was known as the Los Angeles Angels, but when they moved to Anaheim in 1965 they adopted the more generic name, California Angels. In 1997, the Walt Disney Company bought the team and overhauled its stadium,

Quickies

Did you know ...

- that the Detroit Tigers baseball team acquired its name in 1901 when the club's ball players wore yellow-and-black socks? Sports editor Philip Reid thought the socks were similar to those worn by the Princeton University Tigers football team.

changing their name to the Anaheim Angels in order to both benefit from and promote the Anaheim-based Disneyland.

When Arte Moreno took control of the team in 2005, he decided to go for the Los Angeles angle again, but the team's lease with the city of Anaheim stipulated that the word "Anaheim" must be somewhere in the team name. Little did the city expect that Moreno would do what he did: he pushed "Anaheim" to the end, and tacked "Los Angeles" to the beginning, thus giving the team an "official" name that complied with the letter of the lease. In common usage, of course, people would drop the "of Anaheim." The city tried to challenge the name change in court, but dropped their lawsuit in 2009.

Who were the Whiz Kids?

The Philadelphia Phillies had a moderately successful 1949, finishing above .500 — which, for the Phillies in those years, was pretty good. But few saw their 1950 season coming, particularly given the lack of experience on the team. With an average age of 26.4 years, the Phillies were hardly veterans.

But they got off to a tremendous start, and, thanks to performances by the likes of Del Ennis, Richie Ashburn, and 20-game winner Robin Roberts, were able to hold off the Brooklyn Dodgers to win the National League pennant. The media dubbed them "the Whiz Kids," and even after they were swept by the Yankees in the World Series, it looked as though the team had a bright future.

But it was not to be. The following year the Phillies went 73–81, and they would not finish above third place for nearly a quarter century.

They Said It ...

Kiner: "Tell us about your wife. What's her name, and what's she like?"

Coleman: "Her name is Mrs. Coleman, and she likes me."

From an interview between broadcaster Ralph Kiner and the Mets' Choo Choo Coleman.

Why was Hideki Matsui nicknamed "Godzilla" in Japan?

Most people would be flattered to be named for a giant monster — if the nickname came as a result of their ferocious power at the plate. But while Hideki Matsui became a dominant player in Japanese baseball, and later a star in the major leagues, it wasn't his play that earned him the nickname. In his younger days, Matsui suffered from severe acne, and the derogatory nickname referred to his coarse complexion.

Who were the Bash Brothers?

In 1987, the Oakland Athletics emerged as a powerhouse in the American League West, and seemed to be a dynasty in the making. The offensive juggernaut was led by the enormous bats of Jose Canseco and Mark McGwire. Canseco was in only his second full season in the Majors, McGwire his first. Canseco hit 31 home runs, while McGwire set a rookie record with 49.

The show continued the following year when Canseco pounded out a league-leading 42 home runs, backed up by McGwire's 32. It was a historic year for Canseco, who also swiped 40 bases, becoming the first player to hit 40 home runs and steal 40 bases in the same year.

> **They Said It ...**
> "I don't like this 'Bird' thing at all. Markie's not a bird. He's a human being."
> *Mark "The Bird" Fidrych's mother.*

The Bash Brothers remained a potent force until Canseco was traded to the Texas Rangers in 1992. During their years together, they helped lead the A's to three American League pennants and one World Series win.

Who gave Pete Rose the nickname "Charlie Hustle"?

The Charlie Hustle moniker was bestowed on Rose by another baseball great, Mickey Mantle. And like a lot of nicknames, the author of this one was laughing when he first said it.

When Rose was a rookie in 1963, his Reds met Mantle's Yankees in a spring training game. Mantle was watching Rose take batting practice and laughed when Rose, after driving a ball to centre field at the end of his turn in the cage, took off for first base. Mantle ribbed Rose by calling him "Charlie Hustle," and the name stuck.

baseball
media and
popular culture

What trade did George Costanza take George Steinbrenner to task over?

A memorable storyline in the classic series *Seinfeld* features George Costanza taking a job with the New York Yankees. Early in the storyline George boldly criticized Steinbrenner's handling of the team, and he ranted about a trade that had many Yankees fans steaming: the 1988 trade of Jay Buhner to the Seattle Mariners for Ken Phelps. Buhner's outstanding career in Seattle was highlighted by three 40+ home run seasons and a career .852 OPS. Phelps had had an outstanding career of his own, but during his Yankee tenure was a shadow of his former self, and only played parts of two seasons in New York, posting mediocre numbers.

Which major league players played softball for Mr. Burns' team on an episode of *The Simpsons*?

In a February 1992 episode of *The Simpsons*, Homer heroically leads the Springfield Power Plant's softball team to the championship game against the hated rivals from the Shelbyville Power Plant. Springfield owner Mr. Burns is so confident of victory that he bets $1 million on the outcome. To cinch the bet, he hires a group of major league players to work as temporary employees of the Springfield plant, earning spots in the big game.

The players — who are voiced by the real-life players — are: Wade Boggs, Jose Canseco, Roger Clemens, Ken Griffey Jr., Don Mattingly, Steve Sax, Mike Scioscia, Ozzie Smith, and Darryl Strawberry.

Who parodied Terry Cashman's hit "Talkin' Baseball" for an episode of *The Simpsons*?

The classic *Simpsons* episode was memorable not just for the escapades of Homer and the major league players in the body of the episode itself, but for the rib-tickling parody of "Talkin' Baseball" that played during the closing credits. A rarity for *The Simpsons*, the parody was a note-for-note spoof. (*The Simpsons* usually records "similar sounding" tunes for legal reasons).

The parody, "Talkin' Softball," was performed by Terry Cashman himself.

Who threatened to sue the makers of *Field of Dreams* if he was included in the film?

One of the major plots in the 1989 movie *Field of Dreams* involves hero Ray Kinsella kidnapping fictional author Terrence Mann and taking him to a baseball game at Fenway Park in Boston.

The movie is based on the novel *Shoeless Joe* by Canadian author W.P. Kinsella. In the novel, the kidnapped author is real-life recluse J.D. Salinger. Salinger was displeased about Kinsella's use of him as a character, and when the novel was being turned into a Hollywood film, he threatened to sue if his character was included. The film makers didn't want the trouble, and chose to replace the Salinger character with Terrence Mann.

> **They Said It ...**
> "There is no more completely satisfactory drama in literature than the fall of Humpty Dumpty."
> *William DeWolf Hopper on "Casey at the Bat."*

Who wrote "Take Me Out to the Ball Game"?

In 1908, Jack Norworth was riding a subway train in New York City and spotted a sign advertising "Baseball Today — Polo Grounds." He put pen to paper and wrote lyrics about a girl named Katie Casey, a baseball nut who is so enamoured with the sport that when her beau wants to take her to the show, she declines, saying instead that he can "Take me out to the ball game." Albert Von Tilzer provided the music, and the song became an instant vaudeville hit. It later became a part of baseball seventh-inning stretches, though only the chorus is generally played. The original verses have been largely forgotten.

Ironically, the composers of the song were not nearly as baseball mad as the song's heroine. Norworth did not attend his first professional game until 1940, and Von Tilzer only saw his first pro game in 1928.

Who wrote "Casey at the Bat"?

Baseball's best known tragic hero, The Mighty Casey, first appeared in the *San Francisco Examiner* on June 3, 1888. The poem, with the title, "Casey at the Bat: A Ballad of the Republic Sung in the Year 1888," was published in the paper anonymously.

The Original Lyrics to "Take Me Out to the Ball Game"

Katie Casey was baseball mad,
Had the fever and had it bad.
Just to root for the home town crew,
Ev'ry sou Katie blew.
On a Saturday her young beau
Called to see if she'd like to go
To see a show, but Miss Kate said "No,
I'll tell you what you can do:"

Chorus:
Take me out to the ball game,
Take me out with the crowd.
Buy me some peanuts and Cracker Jacks
I don't care if I never get back.
Let me root, root, root for the home team,
If they don't win it's a shame.
For it's one, two, three strikes you're out
At the old ball game.

Katie Casey saw all the games.
Knew the players by their first names.
Told the umpire he was wrong,
All along, good and strong.
When the score was just two to two,
Katie Casey knew what to do,
Just to cheer up the boys she knew,
She made the gang sing this song:
Chorus

Just two months after the poem's publication, it was read on stage for the first time by DeWolf Hopper in the comedy *Prince Methusalem*. The play itself didn't have lasting appeal, but Hopper's recitation of "Casey at the Bat" did, and he would appear more than 10,000 times on stage reciting the poem.

But for years the author of the poem was unknown. Several people tried to take credit until Ernest Lawrence Thayer finally stepped forward and acknowledged that he was the author. The *Examiner* confirmed this claim.

What reporter was snubbed by players when seeking postgame interviews at the 1999 World Series?

As the world approached the end of the 20th century, Major League Baseball decided to mark the event by having fans vote for an All-Century Team. Pete Rose, despite being banned from baseball, was voted to the team and permitted to take part in on-field celebrations prior to Game 2 of the 1999 World Series.

NBC reporter Jim Gray took the opportunity to hound Rose about his past gambling activities. At the time, Rose was still denying that he ever bet on baseball. Gray asked him if he was ready to admit that he bet on baseball, but Rose declined, saying that he'd rather focus on the festivities of the day. But Gray persisted, even after Rose said, several times, that he didn't want to discuss his legal problems.

Fans and players were livid with Gray for his actions to the point that some players decided they would not do post-game interviews with Gray the remainder of the series. New York Yankees outfielder Chad Curtis said as much when Gray tried to corner him for an interview after Game 3. In response to the first question from Gray, Curtis said, "As a team, we kind of decided, because of what happened to Pete, we're not going to talk out here on the field." Curtis then walked off as an embarrassed Gray stood helplessly before the camera and a live TV audience.

Who played in the first televised baseball game?

As was the case with other sports, baseball's first televised game was on an experimental station, W2XBS, which later became WNBC-TV. The college game took place on May 17, 1939, and saw Princeton defeat Columbia 2–1.

The first televised professional game was also on W2XBS later that year on August 26. In fact, it was a double-header. The Brooklyn Dodgers and the Cincinnati Reds split the games, with the Reds winning the first game, 5–2, and the Dodgers taking the nightcap, 6–1. The coverage was crude. There was only one announcer — the legendary Red Barber — and two cameras. One of the cameras showed the play on the field, while the other was focussed on Barber.

Which announcer called Bobby Thomson's home run on television in the 1951 playoff between the Giants and the Dodgers?

The famous call "The Giants win the pennant! The Giants win the pennant!" has tormented Dodgers fans since Bobby Thomson's crushing blow in 1951. However, when the game was live, only those listening on radio heard that call — and even then, they had to be listening to the Giants' "home" coverage. Russ Hodges called the game on the Giants' home radio station, WMCA, while Red Barber called the game on the Dodgers' home station, WMGM.

Those watching on television, however, heard Ernie Harwell call the shot.

In fact, it is pure luck that Hodges' call was ever heard again. The radio station did not record the broadcast. We only have a recording of the call because young Lawrence Goldberg was heading to work that day and asked his mother to record the game on his reel-to-reel tape recorder. Goldberg later presented the tape to Hodges, and now it is impossible to talk about Thomson's home run without referring to Hodges' call.

Who concluded "Chicks dig the longball"?

* that players in the past were more likely to double than to strike out than they are now? In the 1920s, 40 percent of major league players had more doubles than strikeouts. In the 1950s, only 10 percent had more doubles than strikeouts. Now the number is down to 1 percent.

As Mark McGwire was taking aim at Roger Maris's single season home run record in the late 1990s, pitchers couldn't help but feel envious. A Nike commercial played up this professional jealousy with an ad featuring McGwire and Atlanta Braves pitchers Tom Glavine and Greg Maddux. The two hurlers, noticing the attention lavished on McGwire by Heather Locklear, embark on a series of workouts aimed at getting them in shape to do some slugging of their own. After apparently reaching their goals, they finally get Heather's attention, and proclaim, "Chicks dig the longball."

How many of the players predicted to make the Hall of Fame in Terry Cashman's "Talkin' Baseball" actually made it?

Toward the end of the popular 1981 baseball ditty, "Talkin' Baseball," songwriter Terry Cashman introduces then-contemporary names into the chorus, saying that "it's no fluke" that they'll join the other greats in the Hall of Fame. But not all were sure things, as it turns out, and of eight players mentioned, only five were Hall-worthy (Reggie Jackson, Rod Carew, Gaylord Perry, Tom Seaver, and Mike Schmidt), while three had outstanding careers that fell short the Hall (Dan Quisenberry, Steve Garvey, and Vida Blue).

Ten Great Baseball Movies
* *Eight Men Out*
* *Field of Dreams*
* *Bull Durham*
* *The Natural*
* *The Pride of the Yankees*
* *The Bad News Bears*
* *Major League*
* *Bang the Drum Slowly*
* *A League of Their Own*
* *The Bingo Long Traveling All-Stars and Motor Kings*

Who was revealed as the "second spitter" in an incident on an episode of *Seinfeld*?

"The Boyfriend," a 1991 episode of *Seinfeld*, centres around guest star Keith Hernandez, who plays himself. Hernandez is befriended by Jerry, to the dismay of Kramer and Newman, who hold a longstanding grudge against the former Mets first baseman. The pair believe that Hernandez spit at them after Newman taunted him during a spring training game.

Jerry theorizes that Hernandez wasn't the culprit, and that there was a "second spitter." The true cad turns out to be Hernandez's teammate, Roger McDowell.

What was Sam "Mayday" Malone's jersey number?

By the time viewers started seeing Sam Malone's life on the long-running sitcom *Cheers*, his baseball days were long behind him. The fictional former Red Sox pitcher was at one time a top relief pitcher, but had turned to alcohol and, in his own words, "lost [his] curveball."

While his career is barely touched on in the series, there are a few things we can glean. He pitched for the Sox in the mid-1970s, was a poor hitter, and his best-known pitch was his "Slider of Death." (Unfortunately, it was his teammates who gave the pitch its name, after one too many three-run home runs.)

Sam's uniform number was 16. We know this because: a) the number is mentioned in an episode, and b) a picture that is purported to be Sam hangs in the bar, and the player sports the number 16. In fact, the player pictured is Jim Lonborg.

Ten Great Baseball Books

- *Shoeless Joe* by W.P. Kinsella
- *The Glory of Their Time* by Lawrence S. Ritter
- *The Boys of Summer* by Roger Kahn
- *Ball Four* by Jim Bouton
- *The Natural* by Bernard Malamud
- *The Baseball Encyclopedia*
- *The Science of Hitting* by Ted Williams and John Underwood
- *Bums* by Peter Golenbock
- *Only the Ball was White: A History of Legendary Black Players and All-Black Professional Teams* by Robert Peterson
- *Sandy Koufax* by Jane Leavy

When *Cheers* went off the air in 1993, some fans campaigned to have the Red Sox retire the number 16 in Sam's honour. The Red Sox didn't even entertain the suggestion.

Who played Grover Cleveland Alexander in *The Winning Team*?

The film *The Winning Team* depicted the life of Hall of Famer Grover Cleveland Alexander as he battled personal demons (alcoholism), health issues (epilepsy), and the game itself throughout his career. The film, and his career, are highlighted by his three victories over the New York Yankees in the 1926 World Series.

The film is decent, but may have vanished into obscurity had its star not embarked upon a post-acting career. Alexander was played by future-president Ronald Reagan.

Was *The Natural* based on a true story?

While the teams and characters in Bernard Malamud's novel are fictional, there was some inspiration from real life. The novel, and the 1984 film starring Robert Redford, tell the story of Roy Hobbs, a promising young player who is shot by a disturbed woman and has to leave the game, only to return years later to lead his team on a pennant run.

The story bears some resemblance to the story of Eddie Waitkus of the Philadelphia Phillies. In the midst of his second consecutive All-Star season in 1949, Waitkus was shot by an obsessed fan. Though he nearly died, he was able to return the next season as part of the "Whiz Kids" who surprised the National League by winning the pennant.

Similarities between Roy Hobbs and Eddie Waitkus are few. The Hobbs story was inspired by Waitkus's tale, but many of his characteristics as both a player and a person were inspired by other baseball legends, such as Ted Williams, Joe DiMaggio, Shoeless Joe Jackson, and Babe Ruth.

plays, strategies, and statistics

What statistic did the New York Mets lead the National League with in 1962?

Casey Stengel's "Amazing Mets" were anything but amazing in their first season. They lost 120 games, including a 17-game losing streak, had only one hitter bat over .275, and allowed a whopping 968 runs. They finished the season 60½ games out of first place. (That's more than two months of games out of the playoffs.)

With a crew led by such "heroes" as Marvellous Marv Throneberry and 24-game loser Roger Craig, the Mets simply stunk.

But they did lead the league in one stat: most errors.

What position in the batting order produces the most RBIs?

Conventional wisdom is that your big RBI-man is your number four hitter. And conventional wisdom is right on this one, though not as right as you might expect.

In 2008, the number four position on 14 major league teams produced the most RBIs. Close behind, though, was the number three position, which drove in the most runs for 10 teams.

What is OPS?

OPS is, arguably, the best statistic for measuring hitters. "OPS" stands for **O**n-base percentage **P**lus **S**lugging percentage. It measures a hitter's ability to not only to get on base, but also to hit for power. It's also a statistic that is easy to grasp.

Like any stat, it's imperfect. On-base percentage is undervalued — it shouldn't be weighted equally with slugging percentage. Devoted sabermetricians often use formulas to come up with a more OBP-heavy version of OPS. Another imperfection is that some role hitters — such as leadoff men or middle infielders — have low slugging percentages but are major contributors because they get on base at a high rate, and it's unfair, for example, to compare that speedster shortstop's OPS to a slugging first baseman's.

Nonetheless, OPS has taken over as the go-to stat for many fans, and batting average is quickly becoming a secondary statistic.

Where did the word *sabermetrics* come from?

Sabermetrics is the statistical analysis of baseball, and draws its name from the acronym SABR — the Society for American Baseball Research. SABR itself isn't devoted to pure stats — its membership includes many who are more "traditional" baseball researchers and commentators. But the statistical branch of SABR has thrived since the organization was founded in 1971, and Bill James, the grandfather of the modern stats craze, borrowed the name when he coined the word *sabermetrics*.

They Said It ...

"I owe my success to expansion pitching, a short outfield fence, and my hollow bats."

Norm Cash, 1961 batting champion and admitted corker of bats.

Who said, "sabermetrics came from that part of sports writing which consists of analysis, evaluation, opinion, and bullshit"?

Bill James used these words to explain why he pioneered the sabermetric movement in the 1970s. James had grown tired of the tendency of sportswriters to start with a conclusion and then set about to prove that conclusion. According to James, nearly every sportswriter will, for example, say "Player X was the greatest shortstop of all time," and then set about finding supporting arguments. Sabermetricians, on the other hand, start with a question: "Who is the greatest shortstop of all time?" Then they embark on a statistical analysis that comes up with a worthy winner (or at least, worthy according to the criteria the sabermetricians come up with).

Do hitters perform better in short at-bats or long at-bats?

Statistically, batters fare better in short at-bats in terms of batting average and OPS. In 2008, the major league batting average in at-bats of three pitches or less was .301, and the OPS was .784. In long at-bats, the batting average was .223, and the OPS .700.

On-base percentage for longer at-bats was, naturally, higher than for short at-bats, since it's tough to walk a batter on three or fewer pitches.

But proponents of longer at-bats will note a couple of important things that these stats overlook: first, one of the main benefits of long at-bats is that they wear pitchers down, an important result that shouldn't be taken lightly. They'll also tell you that on-base percentage is the most important component of the OPS stat, and the higher OBP for long at-bats — .352 vs. .317 — makes the long at-bat more hitter-friendly.

How good a predictor is the MVP award of future Hall of Fame induction?

One great season does not a career make, but it seems that, in the early years, at least, players who won their league's Most Valuable Player Award were cinches for the Hall of Fame.

Of 18 men named MVP in their respective leagues in the 1930s, only one (Bucky Walters, 1939) did not go on to be a Hall of Famer. Things got less predictable in the next three decades, though with 39 of 60 MVPs from the 1940s, 1950s, and 1960s later being elected to the Hall of Fame, the odds were decent.

Apparently the wheels fell off in the 1970s and 1980s. Of 41 league Most Valuable Players, only 17 are now in Cooperstown. The numbers are putrid in the 1990s (3 of 20), but in fairness, many of the non-Hallers haven't had many (or any) turns on the Hall of Fame ballot, and it may be too early to write them off.

> **Quickies**
> *Did you know ...*
> - that only two players have hit more than 500 career home runs and had a slugging percentage below .500? Eddie Murray had 504 home runs and a .476 SLG. Reggie Jackson had 563 home runs and a .490 SLG.

Do stolen base attempts help or hurt a team?

In the verbal wars between traditionalists and sabermetricians, few arguments are as heated as the To Steal or Not to Steal debate. Traditionalists love the running game; sabermetricians often say that those "caught-stealings" are too damaging, and that you have to have an 80 percent success rate just to avoid a negative impact on your runs scored.

The sabermetricians appear to be right on this count, at least statistically. Even the argument that the threat of a speedy runner on first causes pitchers to be distracted or rush their pitches, thus leading to more success for batters, doesn't hold true when situational stats are used.

On the other hand, even Bill James argues that the 80 percent number should not be set in stone. His own analysis of the 2008 Chicago White Sox, for example, shows that they could actually see benefits from stealing at a mere 57 percent success rate.

Does a high-strikeout pitcher throw more pitches than a low-strikeout pitcher?

It is often said that the downside of striking out a lot of batters is that you end up throwing more pitches, thus wearing yourself out in a game, and taxing your arm long-term. And some pitchers have purposely tried to go for more groundouts than strikeouts in an effort to reduce their pitch counts. But is it true?

On a per-batter basis, yes. Common sense alone tells us that a strikeout generally requires more pitches, and the numbers back us up: the average strikeout requires 4.8 pitches, while the average non-strikeout needs 3.53 pitches.

But on a per-game basis, things are different. Even the average low-strikeout pitcher strikes out about half the number of batters the high-strikeout pitcher does, so those "high" per-at-bat numbers are affecting him, too. And the low-strikeout pitcher also tends to allow more base runners, thus facing more hitters overall. In the end, it comes out about even.

Who is the only player with more than 200 hits in a season, but a mere 25 extra base hits?

While Lloyd Waner amassed an impressive number of hits in 1927 with 223 (and a batting average of .355), his power numbers were underwhelming. He posted only 17 doubles, six triples, and two home runs, good for a .410 slugging percentage — not a high number, considering the number of hits.

> **Quickies**
> *Did you know ...*
> • that the average lifespan of a major league baseball is 5–7 pitches?

What was Babe Ruth's record as a pitcher?

In what was easily the most successful position change ever, Babe Ruth went from the mound to the outfield in order to get the most out of his powerful bat. But while the conversion was, without doubt, the best thing for Ruth and for the game, baseball did lose a solid pitcher with the switch. As a pitcher for the Red Sox, Babe threw for all or part of six seasons, putting together an 89–46 record. As a Yankee, he made a mere five appearances on the mound between 1920 and 1933, but was a perfect 5–0, bringing his lifetime numbers to 94–46 with a 2.28 ERA.

In his first World Series, he pitched 29⅔rds scoreless innings, breaking Christy Mathewson's record and setting a mark that would stand for 43 years.

Whitey Ford was the man who broke that mark, in a bad year for the Babe. It was 1961 — the same year that Ruth's single-season home run record fell. Ford's scoreless innings record eventually reached 33⅔ games before another Yankee, Mariano Rivera, passed it in 2000.

Who invented baseball hand signals?

In 1869, the Cincinnati Red Stockings began using a system of hand signals based on military flag signals which soldiers had used while playing during the civil war period. Baseball hand signals evolved from the very beginning of the game and, consequently, there are many moments and persons involved in their development, but none more important than a 5'4", 148 pound centre fielder named William "Dummy" Hoy.

Hoy was the first deaf baseball player to make the major leagues. One afternoon in 1889, as a centre fielder with the Washington Senators, Hoy set a major league record by throwing out three base runners at home plate. His is a fascinating story, although not recognized in baseball's Hall of Fame. He and his coaches and teammates developed an advanced system of hand gestures to overcome Hoys deafness which was a key impetus in the hand signals evolution. Even umpires began physically indicating the "count" to communicate with Hoy. He couldn't hear the crowd, but Bill Hoy's legacy is a major part of each and every ball game played to this day.

Quickies
Did you know ...
- that the odds of catching a ball at a major league baseball game are 563:1?

William Hoy played 14 years in the majors, retiring in 1902 with a .288 batting average, 2,054 hits, and 726 runs batted in. His 597 stolen bases still ranks 17th in history.

Which is rarer: a perfect game or an unassisted triple play?

Perfect games are rare feats. At the time of publication, only 18 perfect games had been pitched in the history of major league baseball. Given the difficulty of pulling off this feat, it would seem to be the most difficult individual defensive accomplishment in the game.

But there is one feat that is even rarer: the unassisted triple play. Only 13 players have managed to pull off three putouts on their own on a single play.

The two accomplishments are equally rare in the World Series. Each has only been pulled off once. Both times, the Brooklyn Robins/ Dodgers were the victims. In 1920, the Robins' Clarence Mitchell hit a line drive that was caught by Bill Wambsganss of the Cleveland Indians.

Wambsganss caught the ball, touched second to retire the lead runner, and then tagged the runner who had been approaching second. In the 1956 World Series, the Yankees' Don Larsen retired all 27 Dodgers batters to record the only perfect game in the history of postseason baseball.

Which three players have hit 500 or more home runs and also pitched in the major leagues?

The first name that always comes to mind when talking about players who could pitch and hit is Babe Ruth. Ruth started his career as a pitcher, and was converted to a full-time outfielder because his bat was far more valuable than his arm could ever hope to be, and he went on to hit 714 career home runs.

Two other hitting greats also spent time pitching. As one might expect, one of those players only pitched one time in a blowout. In 1940, 21-year-old Ted Williams pitched two innings, giving up a run on three hits with no walks and one strikeout.

Five years later, Jimmie Foxx attempted to become Babe Ruth in reverse. With the end of his playing days in sight, the once mighty slugger was looking for ways to extend his career, and took to the mound. In 1945 he appeared in nine games as a pitcher, posting a 1.59 ERA in 22⅔ innings of work.

Who said, "Anytime you're trying to make statistics tell you who's gonna win the game, that's a bunch of geeks trying to play video games"?

If you want to see grown men come to blows, put second-baseman-turned-broadcaster Joe Morgan in a room with a sabermetrician. Joe Morgan is famous for dismissing statistic-based analysis of the sport. He's even gone as far as to argue against statistical arguments that say he is one of the top two or three second basemen who ever lived.

Who developed the statistic "batting average"?

Henry Chadwick was the Bill James of his day. Baseball's first great statistician, in the 1800s Chadwick developed the box score, earned run average, and batting average. He was also the first to use "K" as an abbreviation for "strikeout."

All of these innovations are still in use today, though batting average has been taking a beating for several years. Most who are well-versed in statistics will say that it is a weak measure that fails to take into account walks and extra base hits, which *are* reflected in other superior measures. At best, batting average is a decent secondary statistic.

So, why did Chadwick develop such a flawed statistic? Chadwick's background was in cricket, and batting average is a very good measure of a cricketer's abilities. Chadwick simply took the cricket formula and applied it in a way more suited to the rules of baseball. Batting average has stuck ever since, and only recent movements have begun drawing fans to more effective statistical measures.

great moments

Who was the last pitcher to win 30 games in a season?

While 30 wins in a season was never commonplace, there was a time when the pitch-till-your-arm-falls-off approach resulted in a number of 30-game winners.

But as coaches and trainers learned to protect valuable arms, pitchers' workloads lessened, and today winning 30 games is a virtual impossibility.

Most impressively, in 1968, Denny McLain won 31 games for the Detroit Tigers, throwing a whopping 336 innings along the way, and posting a sizzling 1.96 ERA.

While thought of today as a one-season wonder, McLain did, in fact, back up that strong performance a year later when he won 24 games with a 2.80 ERA (325 innings) in 1969.

1970 was not so kind. Not only did he go 3–5 with a 4.63 ERA in only 14 starts, but his legal and behavioral issues actually prompted commissioner Bowie Kuhn to suggest he undergo psychiatric counselling. The following year, McLain was able to get a full season in, but went 10–22, leading the league in losses.

Which player hit four inside-the-park home runs in a single game?

Four-homer games are rare, though they have happened; fifteen times, to be exact. But in the "dead ball" era, the longball was hard to come by, and many homers were of the inside-the-park variety. Still, those inside jobs were feats unto themselves.

The most remarkable four-homer game happened on July 13, 1896, when Ed Delahanty of the Philadelphia Quakers had four inside-the-park home runs in a game against the Chicago Colts. Unfortunately, Delahanty's hustle went unrewarded. The Quakers lost the game, 9–8.

Quickies

Did you know ...

- that during a regular nine-inning baseball game, more than 1,000 silent instructions are given — from catcher to pitcher, coach to batter or fielder, fielder to fielder, and umpire to umpire?

Who threw out the ceremonial first pitch on the day that David Cone pitched a perfect game for the New York Yankees in 1999?

July 18, 1999, was Yogi Berra Day at Yankee Stadium. Normally, when a living player is honoured, that player throws out the first pitch. On this occasion, however, since Berra was a legendary Yankee pitcher, it was decided that he would *receive* the first pitch. The man chosen to throw the pitch to Berra was Don Larsen, who had pitched the only perfect game in World Series history.

The game itself overshadowed the pregame festivities, as David Cone pitched a perfect game of his own against the Montreal Expos. It was the first time that a perfect game had been thrown in regular-season interleague play.

In another coincidence involving Larsen, a year earlier, on May 17, 1998, David Wells had also pitched a perfect game for the Yankees. Wells and Larsen were alumni of the same high school.

What is the oldest team in baseball to have never had a pitcher throw a no-hitter?

In major league baseball there are four teams who have gone their entire histories without a single pitcher tossing a no-hitter. Two, the Colorado Rockies and the Tampa Bay Devil Rays/Rays, are relatively recent expansion teams — 1993 and 1998, respectively. The San Diego Padres are also without a no-hitter — they've been around since 1969.

But the New York Mets have lasted the longest without enjoying a no-hitter by one of their hurlers. Established in 1962, the Mets have had a number of pitchers who have gone on to pitch no-hitters with other teams — including the king of the no-hitter himself, Nolan Ryan. Yet none of these pitchers were able to pull off the feat with the Mets.

Players Who Have Hit Four Home Runs in a Game		
Player	Team	Date
Bobby Lowe	Boston Beaneaters	May 30, 1894
Ed Delahanty	Philadelphia Quakers	July 13, 1896
Lou Gehrig	New York Yankees	June 3, 1932
Chuck Klein	Philadelphia Phillies	July 10, 1936
Pat Seerey	Chicago White Sox	July 18, 1948
Gil Hodges	Brooklyn Dodgers	August 31, 1950
Joe Adcock	Milwaukee Braves	July 31, 1954
Rocky Colavito	Cleveland Indians	June 10, 1959
Willie Mays	San Francisco Giants	April 30, 1961
Mike Schmidt	Philadelphia Phillies	April 17, 1976
Bob Horner	Atlanta Braves	July 6, 1986
Mark Whiten	St. Louis Cardinals	September 7, 1993
Mike Cameron	Seattle Mariners	May 2, 2002
Shawn Green	Los Angeles Dodgers	May 23, 2002
Carlos Delgado	Toronto Blue Jays	September 25, 2003

Why were no-hitters more common before 1893?

There was a time in the 19th century when no-hitters and low-hit games were fairly commonplace, and in many years there would be a half dozen or more no-hitters thrown in one of the leagues recognized as "Major" leagues.

But when Bill Hawke of the Baltimore Orioles no-hit the Washington Senators on August 16, 1893, he was the only pitcher that entire year to do so, and no other pitcher threw a no-hitter for more than four years until Cy Young no-hit the Cincinnati Reds on September 18, 1897.

What happened in the game that made no-hitters tougher to come by? The distance from the rubber to home plate changed. In fact, it changed several times in the years prior to 1893. In 1857, the rubber was only 45 feet from home plate. Several years later, the distance was changed to 50 feet. Finally, it was decided that the pitching rubber should be on a direct line between first and third bases, and that meant the pitching rubber was set 60 feet, six inches from home plate, where it remains to this day.

Who is the oldest pitcher to have pitched a no-hitter? Who is the youngest?

It will come as no surprise to most baseball fanatics that Nolan Ryan, at 44 years, eight months, was the oldest man to throw a no-hitter when he overwhelmed the Toronto Blue Jays on May 1, 1991 (striking out 16 batters along the way.)

On the flipside, there is more than one player who can be credited as the youngest member of the no-hit club. While Amos Rusie threw a no-hitter at the age of 20 years, two months in 1891, he did so when the mound was only 50 feet from home plate. In the modern era, the youngest man to throw a no-hitter was John Lush of the Philadelphia Phillies. Despite being a mediocre pitcher, Lush pitched the game of his life when he no-hit the Brooklyn Superbas at the age of 20 years, eight months.

What injuries was Kirk Gibson suffering from when he hit his home run in the 1988 World Series?

Kirk Gibson's dramatic pinch-hit home run in Game 1 of the 1988 World Series was memorable because he was not expected to play due to injury (and, in fact, it was his only plate appearance that series). But few recall what the actual injuries were.

Gibson was suffering from a strained hamstring in his left leg and a sprained ligament in his right leg. To make matters worse, he was battling a stomach virus.

Who gave up Ichiro Suzuki's 100th professional home run?

Ichiro was a star in Japan long before he began making his mark in the major leagues. Though known primarily as a singles hitter, by the time Ichiro played his last game in Japan in 2000, he had well over 100 professional home runs.

They didn't come cheap — Japan being known for pitchers with good arms. In fact, his 100th career home run came against a pitcher who has had success in Japan and North America. Daisuke Matsuzaka — commonly known by his nickname, "Dice-K," surrendered the milestone dinger on July 6, 1999.

What is the name of the trophy given to the winner of the World Series?

Baseball is one of the least trophy-oriented sports. When talking about winning championships, fans and media often use words like "flags" or "pennants" or "rings." And perhaps that's because the trophy that World Series winners receive is so underwhelming. Comprised of a circle of flags, each representing a major league team, it's a difficult trophy to drink champagne out of, and it's not the best item to parade around the field in a victory celebration — there isn't much keeping those flags from snapping off if the trophy is dropped.

And it certainly doesn't help that the trophy has such an uninspiring name: the Commissioner's Trophy.

Why was an NBC cameraman able to catch Carlton Fisk's hand-waving after hitting his game-winning home run in the sixth game of the 1975 World Series?

One of the most memorable broadcast images in baseball is Carlton Fisk, after hitting a 12th-inning fly ball, waving his arms to try to encourage the ball to stay fair, then jumping in the air after it does. But that image shouldn't have been captured at all. Isolated shots of players leaving home plate were uncommon and there were fewer cameras in 1975.

Lou Gerard, the cameraman responsible for the famous footage, would later say that his instructions were to keep his camera on the flight of any ball hit to the outfield. However, he was distracted by a rat nearby, and lost sight of the ball. With nothing to focus on, he kept his camera on Fisk.

> **They Said It ...**
> "People ask me how I'd like to be remembered. I tell them I'd like to be remembered as the guy who hit the line drive over Bobby Richardson's head."
> *From Willie McCovey's Hall of Fame induction speech. (Richardson had snared a McCovey line drive for the final out of the 1962 World Series.)*

Pitchers Who Have Had Perfect Games Spoiled with Two Outs in the Ninth

Date	Pitcher, Team	Batter, Team
July 4, 1908*	Hooks Wiltse, New York Giants	George McQuinlan, Philadelphia Phillies
August 5, 1932	Tommy Bridges, Detroit Tigers	Dave Harris, Washington Senators
June 27, 1958	Billy Pierce, Chicago White Sox	Ed Fitz Gerald, Washington Senators
September 2, 1972**	Milt Pappas, Chicago Cubs	Larry Stahl, San Diego Padres
April 15, 1953	Milt Wilcox, Detroit Tigers	Jerry Hairston Sr., Chicago White Sox
May 2, 1988	Ron Robinson, Cincinnati Reds	Wallace Johnson, Montreal Expos
August 4, 1989	Dave Stieb, Toronto Blue Jays	Roberto Kelly, New York Yankees
April 20, 1990	Brian Holman, Seattle Mariners	Ken Phelps, Oakland Athletics
September 2, 2001	Mike Mussina, New York Yankees	Carl Everett, Boston Red Sox

(*McQuinlan was hit by a pitch. Wiltse ended up with a no-hitter.)

(**Stahl was walked. Pappas ended up with a no-hitter.)

Who was the first pitcher to throw a no-hitter in a game played at a neutral site?

In 2008, Hurricane Ike was bearing down on Texas, and the Houston Astros were forced to move some games out of town while the storm did its damage. So, on September 14, the Astros were the hometown team, but playing out of Milwaukee's Miller Park as the Chicago Cubs came to town.

Despite being a home team living out of suitcases, the Astros thought they might have an edge in the game: the Cubs' pitcher, Carlos Zambrano, was pitching for the first time since suffering rotator cuff tendonitis. But if his shoulder was bothering him, Carlos didn't let it show, pitching a complete-game no-hitter.

blunders, jokes, and not-so-great moments

What position on the New York Mets was known as the Bermuda Triangle of Baseball?

The Mets had many ups and downs between the 1962 expansion and 1987, fielding some of the best and worst teams in baseball history. Their greatest consistency was their inconsistency at third base. During this period — which mostly took place in the time before free agency led to high player turnover — third base was a revolving door. In 26 seasons, 86 different men played third base for the Mets, starting with Don Zimmer. The only iron men — reaching the 250-game plateau (roughly a season and a half worth of work) were Howard Johnson, Hubie Brooks, and Wayne Garrett.

In 1980, someone pointed the dubious trend out to then-third sacker Elliott Maddox. Maddox laughed off the "curse," then, three days later, suffered a season-ending hamstring injury.

How did Daryl Spencer express his frustration with his manager when he played baseball in Japan?

The 1960s saw the beginning of the wave of American players relocating to Japan to become heroes on the other side of the Pacific. Daryl Spencer was among the early arrivals but, like many, had trouble adjusting. Spencer's manager with the Hankyu Braves was livid with Spencer for what he considered a flawed approach to training, and benched Spencer before a game.

Spencer, already miffed, became outraged when, while changing out of his uniform, he heard the stadium announcer listing him among the game's starters: the manager was planning on fooling the opponent into thinking Spencer was playing, then pinch-hitting for him in the first inning.

Spencer waited until it was time for his spot in the order to be on deck, then stormed out of the dressing room into the on-deck circle to "warm up," wearing nothing but his underwear. He was fined $200.

What situation involving George Steinbrenner became known as "The Elevator Incident"?

During the 1981 World Series between the Yankees and Dodgers, George III was on an elevator in Los Angeles with two Dodgers fans. The fans began taunting him and one threw a beer bottle at the Yankees' owner. George easily fought off his attackers with a couple of swift blows that sent them scurrying for the hallway at the next floor.

At least, that's the story that George told the media.

Doubts were immediately cast on Steinbrenner's story, since there were no witnesses, and the image of Super George fighting evil with his mighty fists seemed implausible. One of the men George supposedly disposed of came forward, and said that George punched the elevator door in frustration, but didn't lay a finger on them.

Even George's peers questioned George's tale. The owner of the Baltimore Orioles — lawyer Edward Bennett Williams — said that if George's story were true, "this is the first time a millionaire has ever hit someone and not been sued."

> **They Said It ...**
> "In [John] McGraw I at last discovered the real and authentic Most Remarkable Man in America." *George Bernard Shaw.*

Who won a Gold Glove as a designated hitter?

The Gold Glove Awards have often been criticized for favouring players who are strong offensively, despite the fact that the Gold Glove is meant for defensive excellence only.

Never was this criticism more severe than when Rafael Palmeiro won the 1999 American League Gold Glove at first base. Palmeiro, who had an excellent offensive season, hitting 47 home runs with a .324 batting average, didn't embarrass himself at first ... but then again, he didn't have much opportunity to do so. He only played 28 games at first that year. He played 135 games at his primary position, but defence wasn't really a requirement. Palmeiro was a designated hitter.

Which major league team wore shorts?

It's hard to imagine what drove the Chicago White Sox to play in shorts in 1976, but with Bill Veeck as owner nothing should have come as a surprise.

The White Sox were already making questionable uniform choices, having adopted collared shirts. But on August 8, 1976, the Sox went a step further when facing the Kansas City Royals in a double-header. The White Sox took to the field in shorts that came halfway down their thighs. Not only were shorts impractical in a sport that involves players sliding on dirt, grass, and AstroTurf — they were also ugly.

The Royals' John Mayberry mocked the Sox players, saying "You guys are the sweetest team we've ever seen." The Sox changed into long pants for the second game of the double-header, and never wore shorts again.

How did Bob Gibson deal with reporters' questions about his injury in 1967?

Legendary pitcher Bob Gibson suffered a broken leg at the worst possible time: in the middle of a pennant race. It's no wonder that St. Louis Cardinals sports writers were anxious to know when he'd return. But their repeated inquiries began to irk Gibson while on the road to recovery. Gibson, never one to be warm and fuzzy with the media, let them know that his patience had run out. To avoid the predictable exchange, he taped a piece of paper to his shirt. It read: "1. Yes, it's off. 2. No, it doesn't hurt. 3. I don't know how much longer."

> **Quickies**
> *Did you know ...*
> - that Jeff Cirillo is the only player to have more than 400 hits for both the Milwaukee Brewers in each league? He had 472 hits for the Brewers before the team moved to the National League, and 528 wins after.

Who was the general manager of the Chicago White Sox in 1986?

A number of teams have hired broadcasters to be field managers, but the Chicago White Sox made a decision they would quickly regret when they brought Hawk Harrelson out of the broadcast booth to be their GM after the 1985 season.

Harrelson made the questionable decision to release the organization's minor league managers and replace them with former major league players. His theory was that players would listen to someone who had "been there." He converted future Hall of Fame catcher Carlton Fisk into a left fielder, saying "He can run, and has a heck of an arm," as if that were all there were to playing left field. The move was made to clear the way for the light-hitting but defensively sound Joel Skinner, who was making a meteoric rise from "unknown" to "little known."

In June of 1986, the White Sox were in fourth place in the AL West. Harrelson fired the manager — some guy named Tony La Russa. La Russa was subsequently hired by the fifth-place Oakland Athletics, who were eight games behind the Sox. By season's end, the A's had climbed to third place, the Sox were in dead last, and Hawk was out of a job.

Perhaps there are some things you shouldn't put on the board.

> **They Said It ...**
> "He told me that he would give up all his money and just about everything else he's got if the fellows he played with and against would only accept him and talk to him today."
> *Paul Krichell, scout, recalling a conversation with a long-retired Ty Cobb.*

Who did the Tampa Bay Devil Rays select fifth overall in the 1997 expansion draft?

By 2008 the Rays had built a solid team after finishing last almost every season of their existence then drafting well with good draft positions. And they even got off to a good start as drafters in the 1997 expansion draft.

But trading players has not always been their strong suit, and such was the case with their fifth-overall pick in '97. The Rays drafted Bobby Abreu, then immediately traded him to the Philadelphia Phillies for Kevin Stocker.

Stocker had been a solid player in his brief career, but after joining the Rays, his career went steadily downhill and he last played in 2000. Abreu, meanwhile, was a two-time all-star, a Gold Glove winner, and had an OPS that hovered around the .900 mark year-in, year-out.

Who said "I'm a little fatigued" in the middle of Game 7 of the 2003 ALCS?

With his team up by three runs over the Yankees through six, Boston Red Sox hurler Pedro Martinez appeared to be cruising along. In the dugout, he confessed to the team's assistant trainer that he was feeling "a little fatigued," but he continued to throw in the seventh, giving up a home run to Jason Giambi.

In the eighth inning, the Sox again up by three, the wheels came off. Derek Jeter doubled. Bernie Williams singled him home. The fatigue was evident to most observers, and perhaps even to Sox manager Grady Little, who came to the mound and asked Pedro if he was okay to continue. Pedro said "yes," and Little, to the surprise of even the broadcasters, listened. He left Martinez in.

By the time Little finally pulled Martinez a batter later, the game was tied, and what had seemed like a sure trip to the World Series was decided in the 11th inning when Aaron Boone homered to give the Yankees the win, prolonging the Sox' curse.

Quickies
Did you know ...
- that veteran umpire Ron Luciano once played third base during a spring training game? Luciano was ribbing Buddy Bell about two errors he had made, and Bell challenged Luciano to take over at third while Bell umpired. Luciano agreed, and during his one inning in the field he fielded a ground ball cleanly then threw to second. His throw was not only high, but the runner was clearly safe by a fair margin. Fellow umpire Joe Brinkman called the runner out.

How did the Boston Red Sox finish a half game behind the Detroit Tigers in 1972, despite both teams playing every scheduled game?

The 1972 baseball season was historic for the wrong reasons. It was the first year that league play was interrupted by a players' strike. The strike pushed back the start of the season until April 15. The owners tried to come up with a solution to the lost games, and came up with a solution that virtually every observer thought was absurd: the missed games would simply be wiped out, and the season would pick up with the games regularly scheduled for that date.

> **Quickies**
> *Did you know ...*
> • that Ty Cobb became wealthy through Coca-Cola? He began promoting the company as a player and was one of its early investors. By the time he died in 1961, Cobb owned 20,000 shares in the soft drink giant.

This meant that teams competing for the same division titles were playing a different number of games. In three of the four divisions this wasn't an issue, as the champion teams had sizeable leads at season's end. But in the American League East, the Red Sox had played only 155 games, while the Tigers had played 156. That one game was critical, as a single Red Sox win would have put them into a tie with the Tigers.

What could possibly go wrong at a 10-cent beer night?

Apparently the 1974 Cleveland Indians failed to ask themselves that question. Or if they did, they didn't think too long about the answer.

After a terrible 1973 season (71–91, good for last in the AL East), the Indians weren't expected to contend in 1974, and were happy to be hovering near the .500 mark. In an effort to draw fans, the Indians came up with the 10-cent beer scheme. "Beer Night," needless to say, was well-received by fans, who flocked to the ballpark (25,000 fans being considered sizeable in those days) to take advantage of the Tribe's largesse.

Around the sixth inning, fans had consumed a fair bit of the affordable offering, and several expressed their gratitude by running onto the field. Things took a more dangerous turn, though, when two fans ran after Texas Rangers outfielder Jeff Burroughs and attempted to steal his hat. They were followed by several dozen other crazies who scuffled with players from both teams. The introduction of a folding chair into the melee was decidedly unwelcome. Nine arrests later, the game was called and the Indians were forced to forfeit.

There was no Beer Night II.

What did Chicago sports broadcaster Chet Coppock call "the dumbest single coaching situation in the history of modern sports"?

The sad-sack Chicago Cubs weren't striking fear into the hearts of opponents on the field in the 1950s and early 1960s, so perhaps owner Phil Wrigley and GM El Tappe thought they'd dazzle competitors with their brilliance as innovators. In 1962, they decided that they'd do away with managers and instead implement a rotating coaching system that saw different men serve as head coach throughout the season. Seriously.

The idea was that there would be eight coaches — four at the major league level at any given time and four at the minor league level. The coaches would rotate between the major and minor leagues, and one of these rotating coaches would be the "manager." Who managed when seemed to be an arbitrary decision.

> **They Said It ...**
> "I don't room with him, I room with his suitcases."
> *Ping Bodie, roommate of Babe Ruth.*

Few belief systems were destroyed when the experiment turned out to be an utter disaster. The so-called "College of Coaches" was abandoned after one year, and the Cubs returned to losing the old fashioned way.

Who was blown off the mound at the 1961 All-Star Game?

The arrival of the former New York Giants in San Francisco in 1958 created the need for a true baseball stadium, and plans were set in motion to build Candlestick Park. The park took its name from its location on Candlestick Point, which was noted for, among other things, high winds, particularly in the afternoon hours (when most baseball games were played in those days).

The swirling winds made games at the Stick a miserable, chilly occasion at times. One of the most infamous moments occurred during the 1961 All-Star Game when pitcher Stu Miller was hit by a gust of wind so strong that it actually blew him off the pitching rubber. Apparently local knowledge wasn't much help — Miller was a Giants pitcher.

What was the "Boston Massacre"?

In midsummer, 1978, the Boston Red Sox had a seemingly insurmountable 14-game lead over the second-place New York Yankees. Over the next 49 games, the Sox posted a respectable, though unspectacular, 25–24 record while the Yanks went on a 35–14 tear to close within four games. The rivals met on September 7 for the first game of a four-game series at Fenway.

> **They Said It ...**
> "You can draw more people to a losing team, plus bread and circuses, than a losing team and a long, still silence."
> *Bill Veeck.*

The series was brutal. The Yankees won all four games by scores of 15–3, 13–2, 7–0, and 7–4, and the teams were tied. At season's end they remained tied, and the Yankees won a one-game playoff, thanks to the heroics of Bucky Dent. But while Dent's home run was the final nail in the coffin, the sweep that came to be known as the Boston Massacre remains a bitter piece of Red Sox lore.

How did a catcher's mask influence the outcome of the 1924 World Series?

The final tilt of the 1924 World Series between the New York Giants and the Washington Senators came down to an exciting Game 7. At the end of nine innings, the teams were knotted at three runs apiece, forcing extra innings. In the bottom of the 12th, Muddy Ruel led off for Washington and popped the ball into foul territory behind the plate.

The normally reliable Giants catcher, Hank Gowdy, whipped off his mask and threw it to the ground, then attempted to position himself to catch the pop-up. Unfortunately, when he threw the mask to the ground, he threw it directly in his own path, and stuck his foot in the mask as he circled back.

Waiting for the ball to come down, Gowdy tried in vain to kick the mask free. He failed in the attempt — and also failed to catch the ball.

On the next pitch, Ruel doubled and then scored on a single by Earl McNeely to win the World Series.

How was the last out of the 1926 World Series recorded?

The New York Yankees were in a tight battle in the seventh and final game of the World Series against the St. Louis Cardinals, trailing 3–1 going into the ninth inning. But they had hope: Babe Ruth was scheduled to bat third in the inning, followed by Bob Meusel and Lou Gehrig. So, even after the Cards' Grover Cleveland Alexander recorded the first two outs, the heart of the order was ready to save the day.

Ruth appeared to do his part, walking on four pitches to bring the tying run to the plate with two outs. But as Alexander wound up to throw to Meusel, Ruth did the unthinkable: he took off for second. Catcher Bob O'Farrell, able to restrain his glee (and perhaps his laughter) fired the ball to second for an easy putout as Ruth ran his team out of the inning, and the World Series.

> **They Said It ...**
> "Do you think I can manage? I have all the credentials, you know. I can really run a game, run a team. I'll do it someday. You'll see."
> *Billy Martin, age 21, in 1950.*

Why did the Oakland Athletics' Mike Andrews miss Game 3 of the 1973 World Series?

Andrews had had a nightmarish 12th inning in Game 2. He made two errors that allowed the New York Mets to score the game-winning run. But the nightmare was shared by the A's owner, Charles Finley. Finley was so angry with Andrews that he wanted him removed from the roster for the remainder of the series. But he also wanted to be able to fill Andrews' roster spot with another player, so he convinced the team doctor to sign a letter stating that Andrews had a shoulder injury and could not play.

Commissioner Bowie Kuhn refused to give credence to the letter unless it was co-signed by Andrews himself. The completely healthy Andrews wanted to play, and initially refused to sign. However, Finley bullied him into putting pen to paper, and Andrews was, temporarily, out of the series. He did not play Game 3.

The Athletics players were outraged at the way their teammate was being treated, and several threatened to refuse to play if Andrews was forced to fake an injury and miss the Series. Kuhn eventually stepped in and forced Finley to allow Andrews back on the roster. In Game 4 in New York, Mets fans gave Andrews a standing ovation when he came up for his first at-bat.

What marred Ken Johnson's no-hitter for the Houston Colt .45s in 1964?

Ken Johnson had had modest success in his professional career, and on most days could look forward to being nothing more than a capable arm. But on April 23, 1964, against the Cincinatti Reds, everything came together as Johnson pitched the game of his life. In a complete, nine-inning outing, he did not allow a single hit. But in the ninth inning, he committed a throwing error on a bunted ball by Pete Rose. Rose ended up on second. A groundout and another error later, Rose scored.

In the meantime, Reds starter Joe Nuxhall pitched a shutout. Ken Johnson became the first and, to date, the only pitcher to throw a no-hitter and lose.

What was the umpire's ruling when Randy Johnson hit a bird with a pitch?

One of the strangest incidents of freak accidents in baseball history took place on March 24, 2001. Arizona Diamondback pitcher Randy Johnson, one of the most feared fireballers in the game, was pitching to the San Francisco Giants' Calvin Murray. Johnson wound up, threw the ball, and suddenly the ball's progress toward the plate was halted in an explosion of feathers. A dove had chosen the wrong moment to cross the Big Unit's path.

The dead bird was hit so hard that it flew over the head of catcher Rod Barajas. The ball never made it to the play.

So, what call does the umpire make? No pitch.

While many found the incident amusing, Johnson himself was a bit shaken. After the game, he was quoted as saying "I didn't think it was all that funny."

Who was the only player in major league history to have a fraction for a uniform number?

Bill Veeck was legendary for crazy ideas aimed at generating headlines and promoting his teams. In 1951 he was owner of the struggling St. Louis Browns, and decided a little excitement was needed. He came up with one of his most memorable ideas: signing a player named Eddie Gaedel.

No one had ever heard of Gaedel, but after his first and only plate appearance on August 19 against the Detroit Tigers, no one would ever forget him. At 3'7", the 26-year-old dwarf was the shortest player ever to play in the majors. Veeck had Browns manager Zack Taylor bring Gaedel up as a pinch-hitter in the first inning. Tigers pitcher Bob Cain couldn't find the tiny strike zone, and Gaedel walked on four pitches. He was replaced by a pinch-runner, and his career was over — with an impressive 1.000 OBP.

To add to the amusement, Veeck gave Gaedel the uniform number 1/8.

What did Canton receive in return when they traded Cy Young to the Cleveland Spiders in 1890?

Cy Young would go on to become the most successful pitcher in baseball history, with an amazing 511 career victories, but apparently the Canton team wasn't fully aware of his value. When the Cleveland Spiders began salivating over the prospect of acquiring the young pitcher, the asking price turned out to be more than affordable. The Spiders received Cy Young and Canton's owner received a tailored suit.

This was, arguably, the worst deal in the history of the game — though there are a couple of players who might say otherwise. Minor leaguer Jack Fenton may not have had Young's greatness, but surely being traded for a box of prunes was a massive overpayment. And Mike Dondero may not have been destined for the Hall of Fame, but surely when he was traded by his team, a farm team of the St. Louis Browns, he could have commanded more than a dozen doughnuts.

What did Pete Rose do to give the National League a psychological edge over the American League in the 1978 All-Star Game?

During the 1970s, the National League was dominating the American League in All-Star Games, and they were seen as the clear favourites going into the 1978 matchup. Pete Rose decided to take advantage of the perception that the NL was the superior league. Rose bought several dozen balls made by Mizuno. The balls were more tightly wound, which allowed them to travel much further when hit. Rose smuggled the balls in for the National League's portion of batting practice, and the NL All-Stars teed off, hitting shot after shot into the outfield stands at San Diego Stadium.

The American League players were in awe of the power display.

When the NL was finished, the balls were gathered up and replaced with the official league-approved balls, and the American League All-Stars couldn't match their counterparts' prowess.

Did it help? Well, the National League won the game 7–3, but they were expected to win all along. At the very least, it didn't hurt.

How did Pepper Martin defend against the bunt during a 1938 game against the Boston Braves?

The St. Louis Cardinals' Pepper Martin hated to field bunts when he played third base, and was already known to punish the occasional bunter by throwing the ball at them after fielding it.

Before a 1938 game against the Boston Braves, Martin approached the Braves' manager, Casey Stengel, and warned him not to let his players bunt. Casey, of course, immediately instructed his players to bunt to Martin as often as possible.

In response, Martin began throwing not at the first baseman, but at the runners' heads.

Eventually, the tactic took a toll. Elbie Fletcher came to the plate for the Braves and hit down a bunt. As soon as a seething Martin moved to field it, Fletcher ran … towards the dugout, fearing for his life. Martin then threw the ball into the Braves' dugout, scattering the players.

It was the last time a Brave tried to bunt to Martin that day.

What is Steve Blass Disease?

Also known as Chuck Knoblauch Disease, this is the kind of "disease" you don't want to have named after you. The affliction is a mental one: the suffering player has a penchant for making wild throws for no apparent reason. Blass became infamous for a mental block that caused him to throw wild pitches at the worst possible moments.

Knoblauch's affliction was more dire. A one-time Gold Glover at second base, something in Chuck's head clicked the wrong way mid-career and his errant throws became commonplace. He had to be moved to the outfield to avoid the mind-blowing problem.

Perhaps the most dramatic change made to a player with this problem was Rick Ankiel. A solid pitcher just emerging in the NL, he had a strong season in 2000, going 11–7 with a 3.50 ERA. But Ankiel suddenly developed a problem with throwing wild pitches. The problem was so bad that he had to give up pitching entirely, and was converted into an outfielder. The unlikely result was that Ankiel was able to work his way back to the Majors with his bat, and actually enjoyed a fair bit of success, hitting 25 home runs in 2008.

firsts and record-breakers

Who is the only player to lead his league in hits for three different teams?

Over the course of his career, Paul Molitor was a consistent hitting machine who found success everywhere he went. A long-time Milwaukee Brewer, Molitor first topped the American League in hits in 1991 when he hit safely 216 times. Two years later he helped lead the Toronto Blue Jays to their second consecutive World Series with a league-leading 211 hits. And finally, Molitor was a Minnesota Twin when he topped the American League with 225 hits in 1996.

Which Most Valuable Player posted the lowest batting average of all MVPs — a measly .267?

With a batting average that low, one would expect the player in question to be someone who put on an incredible display of power — a Roger Maris or a Mark McGwire. But the 1944 National League MVP, the St. Louis Cardinals' Marty Marion, did little that was historic en route to winning the award. He provided passable offence (his OBP of .324 was something his team could live with) and outstanding defence at shortstop.

Marion never became a strong hitter, though on occasion he did manage to get on base at a healthy clip. But his career revolved around his defence, and while he never won the MVP award again, he did make seven all-star teams.

Which catcher has caught the most 20-game winners?

While the catcher plays an important role in calling pitches and handling pitchers over the course of a game, a 20-game winner is likely to be a darn good pitcher regardless of who his catcher is. Still, catching multiple 20-game winners is an accomplishment for any backstop.

Jim Hegan of the Cleveland Indians holds the distinction of being the primary catcher for the most 20-win seasons. The pitchers doing the heavy labour were Bob Feller (three times), Bob Lemon (seven times),

Twenty-Three Players Who Hit More Than 30 Home Runs in Their Rookie Season		
Year	Player, Team	Home Runs
1930	Wally Berger, Boston Braves	38
1934	Hal Trosky, Cleveland Indians	35
1937	Rudy York, Detroit Tigers	35
1939	Ted Williams, Boston Red Sox	31
1950	Al Rosen, Cleveland Indians	37
	Walt Dropo, Boston Red Sox	34
1956	Frank Robinson, Cincinnati Reds	38
1959	Bobby Allison, Washington Senators	30
1963	Jimmie Hall, Minnesota Twins	33
1964	Tony Oliva, Minnesota Twins	32
	Jim Ray Hart, San Francisco Giants	31
1971	Earl Williams, Atlanta Braves	33
	Willie Montanez, Philadelphia Phillies	30
1983	Ron Kittle, Chicago White Sox	35
1986	Jose Canseco, Oakland Athletics	33
1986	Pete Incaviglia, Texas Rangers	30
1987	Mark McGwire, Oakland Athletics	49
	Matt Nokes, Detroit Tigers	32
1993	Mike Piazza, Los Angeles Dodgers	35
	Tim Salmon, California Angels	31
1997	Nomar Garciaparra, Boston Red Sox	30
2001	Albert Pujols, St. Louis Cardinals	37
2007	Ryan Braun, Milwaukee Brewers	34

Gene Bearden (once), Early Wynn (four times), Mike Garcia (twice), and Herb Score (once). That's 18 times. He also caught for two other 20-game winners, but was not the primary catcher those seasons.

Catchers Who Have Caught Three or More No-Hitters		
Player	Team	No-Hitters
Jason Varitek	Boston Red Sox	4
Ray Schalk	Chicago White Sox	3
Alan Ashby	Houston Astros	3
Yogi Berra	New York Yankees	3
Roy Campanella	Brooklyn Dodgers	3
Bill Carrigan	Boston Red Sox	3
Del Crandall	Milwaukee Braves	3
Lou Criger	Boston Red Sox	3
Johnny Edwards	Cincinnati Reds	3
Silver Flint	Chicago Cubs	3
Jim Hegan	Cleveland Indians	3
Charles Johnson	Florida Marlins	3
Ed McFarland	Philadelphia Phillies/Chicago White Sox	3
Val Picinich	Philadelphia Athletics/Washington Senators/Boston Red Sox	3
Luke Sewell	Cleveland Indians/Chicago White Sox	3
Jeff Torborg	Los Angeles Dodgers/California Angels	3

Which catcher has caught the most no-hitters?

Catchers take pride in catching no-hitters. Any time a pitcher is so dominant that not a single batter is able to earn a hit, the catcher has made a good call or two along the way. (You don't see a lot of pitchers shaking off their catchers en route to a no-hitter.)

The all-time leader in no-hitters caught is Jason Varitek of the Boston Red Sox. Varitek has caught four no-hitters. That edges out 15 catchers, all of whom have caught three no-hitters.

Which pitchers have pitched no-hitters and led their leagues in saves?

A number of pitchers have enjoyed success as starters and relievers, but only three have achieved the height of starting dominance (the no-hitter) and the saves crown. Dave Righetti of the New York Yankees threw a no-hitter in 1983, then three years later became the first man with a no-hitter to his credit to also lead his league in saves as a reliever when he had 46 saves.

Dennis Eckersley, who had thrown a no-hitter for the Cleveland Indians in 1977, became the second man to pull off the double when he was a dominant reliever for the Oakland Athletics in 1988, saving 45 games. (Eckersley also led the AL in saves in 1992.)

Derek Lowe of the Boston Red Sox went in the other direction, leading the AL with 42 saves in 2000, then throwing a no-hitter as a starter in 2002.

> **Quickies**
> *Did you know ...*
> • that outfielder Joel Youngblood once had hits for two different teams in two different cities on the same day? On August 4, 1982, Youngblood was playing an afternoon game for the New York Mets at Chicago's Wrigley Field when he drove in two runs with a single in the third inning off Ferguson Jenkins. Before the game ended, he was traded to the Montreal Expos, and he was pulled from the lineup. He hopped on a plane to join the Expos for their night game against the Phillies in Philadelphia. In the seventh inning he hit a single off Steve Carlton.

Who was the 3,000th strikeout victim of two different pitchers?

Cesar Geronimo was not a superstar hitter, but put up some decent numbers during his 15-year career, inlcuding being a defensive star and winning four gold gloves. So, he's better known as a quality player than as a footnote to history.

And yet, he was a special footnote to history on two occasions. On July 17, 1974, Geronimo became Bob Gibson's 3,000th strikeout victim. Then on July 4, 1980, he became the only man to be the 3,000th K for two different pitchers when he was fanned once again by Nolan Ryan.

Which two players were the most prolific home-run duo while members of the same team?

Having one master slugger is one thing, but to bring together two players with tremendous home-run prowess is something most teams dream about. So, the Milwaukee Braves were the envy of baseball when they had Hank Aaron and Eddie Mathews in their lineup. The two were teammates for the Braves in Milwaukee and, when the Braves moved, Atlanta, from 1954 to 1966. During that time Aaron hit 442 home runs, while Mathews hit 421 for a combined 863 round trips.

Players with 200+ Home Runs in Both the AL and NL
- Frank Robinson
- Fred McGriff
- Mark McGwire
- Ken Griffey Jr.

Their nearest competitors, unsurprisingly, are Babe Ruth (498) and Lou Gehrig (348), whose 846 combined homers as teammates covered the years 1923–34.

Who was the only team *not* shut out by Bob Gibson in 1968?

Always a dominant pitcher, Bob Gibson took his game to another level in his memorable 1968 season. He was almost unhittable, and posted the lowest ERA in big league history at 1.12.

In 34 starts he only failed to go the distance six times. The incredible season was highlighted by a phenomenal 13 shutouts. In fact, at some point in the season he shut out each and every team in the National League (then later shut out the Detroit Tigers in the World Series). The only team to avoid the goose egg were the Los Angeles Dodgers, though Gibson held them to a single run on two occasions.

Quickies
Did you know ...
- that Todd Zeile homered for more teams than any other player? During his 16-year career, Zeile managed to hook up with 11 organizations, hitting home runs for each team. The beneficiaries of Zeile's power were the St. Louis Cardinals (1989–95), Chicago Cubs (1995), Philadelphia Phillies (1996), Baltimore Orioles (also 1996), Los Angeles Dodgers (1997–98), Florida Marlins (1998), Texas Rangers (1998–99), New York Mets (2000–01, 2004), Colorado Rockies (2002), New York Yankees (2003), and Montreal Expos (2004).

Which two players have played in three consecutive World Series with three different teams?

The 1980s saw baseball players move from team to team more than ever before, thanks in large part to the opening of the free agent floodgates early in the decade. Don Baylor managed to work his way onto three top teams in the 1980s via trade and free agency, and might be the poster boy for the new era of revolving doors. In 1986, he was part of the Boston Red Sox squad that played in, and lost, the World Series. The following year, he joined the Minnesota Twins and won the first and only World Series of his career. And finally, in 1988, he returned to the Oakland Athletics (one of his many former teams) and travelled to the Fall Classic one more time.

Baylor stood alone in the three-Series-three-teams club until 2009, when Eric Hinske was added to the New York Yankees World Series roster after being left out of the League Championship Series. Previously, he'd been a member of the 2007 World Champion Red Sox and the 2008 American League Champion Tampa Bay Rays.

> **Players with 200-Hit Seasons in Both the AL and NL**
> - George Sisler (St. Louis Browns, AL, 1920, 1921, 1922, 1925, 1927; Boston Braves, NL, 1929)
> - Al Oliver (Texas Rangers, AL, 1980; Montreal Expos, NL, 1982)
> - Bill Buckner (Chicago Cubs, NL, 1982; Boston Red Sox, AL, 1985)
> - Steve Sax (Los Angeles Dodgers, NL, 1986; New York Yankees, AL, 1989)
> - Vladimir Guerrero (Montreal Expos, NL, 1998, 2002; Anaheim/Los Angeles Angels, AL, 2004, 2006)

Who holds the record for most strikeouts in a game by a relief pitcher?

On July 18, 2001, Curt Schilling of the Arizona Diamondbacks started a game at San Diego's Qualcomm Stadium. A power failure forced the game to be suspended, and play resumed in the second inning the following day. Randy Johnson took the mound that day, and while for all intents and purposes his outing was treated like any other start, his appearance technically qualifies as a relief appearance.

Johnson struck out 16 batters in the outing — impressive for a start, and record-shattering for relief.

Who was the first catcher to lead his league in triples?

Catchers are rarely speedsters on the base paths, and most don't have many triples to their credit. It's rare for a catcher to lead the league in triples. In fact, it's only happened twice.

Tim McCarver, better known to younger fans for his work as a colour television commentator, was one of the better catchers in his day, and in 1966 with the St. Louis Cardinals he hit 13 three-baggers as part of his first all-star season. He never had more than seven triples in any other season of his career, but did continue to "run well for a catcher."

The other catcher to be a lead-leader in triples was Carlton Fisk, who tied for the lead with nine triples for the 1972 Boston Red Sox.

Who is the only pitcher to win World Series games with three different teams?

Players Who Have Won Batting Titles for Two Different Clubs

- Nap Lajoie: Philadelphia Athletics (1901) and Cleveland Indians (1902, 1903, 1904, 1910)
- Rogers Hornsby: St. Louis Cardinals (1920–25) and Boston Braves (1928)
- Lefty O'Doul: Philadelphia Phillies (1929) and Brooklyn Dodgers (1932)
- Jimmy Foxx: Philadelphia Athletics (1933) and Boston Red Sox (1938)
- Ernie Lombardi: Cincinnati Reds (1938) and Boston Braves (1942)
- Bill Madlock: Chicago Cubs (1975, 1976) and Pittsburgh Pirates (1981, 1983)

While nearly two dozen pitchers have won World Series outings for two teams, only one player has done so with three teams. In 1993, Curt Schilling was outstanding for the Philadelphia Phillies, winning Game 5 against the Blue Jays to force a Game 6 (which the Jays won). Eight years later, in 2001, he had a win in three starts to help the Arizona Diamondbacks win their first title. And he posted single wins in both the 2004 and 2007 Series for the Boston Red Sox — the last victory coming at the age of 40 in his final career appearance.

the greats
and near-greats

Who are the only two managers who have won World Championships in the American League and National League?

Sparky Anderson led the Big Red Machine — the Cincinnati Reds — to back to back world titles in 1975 and 1976. Later, he moved to the American League as manager of the Detroit Tigers. In 1984 the Tigers tore up baseball, winning 35 of their first 40 games and cruising to a division title. They then marched through the playoffs, sweeping the Kansas City Royals to win the AL pennant, then humbling the San Diego Padres four games to one.

Five years later, Tony LaRussa won his first World Series as manager of the 1989 Oakland Athletics. He later managed the 2006 World Champion St. Louis Cardinals.

Which pitcher admitted late in his career that he should have been a hitter like his brother?

Poor Ken Brett was known for much of his career as "George's brother," but growing up Ken was actually the better hitter of the two. But Ken also had a golden arm, and as a professional focused on pitching (though he did hit well at the plate at times, once homering in four straight games).

Ken Brett had some decent years, reaching double digits in wins on four occasions, but also had some struggles and battled a number of injuries. He was a serviceable starter, but never a star in his 14 big-league seasons. George, meanwhile, enjoyed a Hall of Fame career with the Kansas City Royals.

Late in his career Brett was asked if, given the chance to relive his career, he'd choose to be an outfielder instead of a pitcher. He replied, "Absolutely. I know now that's what I should have done."

118

What broadcaster set a record by calling every game in a team's history for 27 years, starting from the time they first took the field?

Many broadcasters have been iron-men, but Tom Cheek's streak was phenomenal. Cheek called the first game ever played by the Toronto Blue Jays on April 7, 1977, and then continued to call every single game until June 3, 2004, which equalled to 4,303 games. Over that time he saw the Jays rise from struggling newcomers to World Champions, and called some of the most memorable moments in baseball history. His call of Joe Carter's World Series-winning home run in 1993 is the go-to sound bite for Toronto baseball fans.

Cheek nearly ended the streak a couple of times along the way. A dental emergency almost sidelined him in the 1980s, and his daughter had to talk him out of attending her college graduation in the 1990s. (Cheek would later say that he regretted listening to her.) Ultimately, Cheek took his first day off to attend the funeral of his father.

> **They Said It …**
> "If I go to Nicaragua, the stealing will stop. They would not dare steal from Roberto Clemente."
> *Roberto Clemente, prior to boarding his doomed flight to aid earthquake victims in Nicaragua.*

Which two "Carls" played for the Lake Ronkonkoma Cardinals until 1958?

The Lake Ronkonkoma Cardinals were a semi-pro team that would not otherwise be noteworthy, except that in the late 1950s they featured a father-son duo that was something special. Carl Sr. played third base and hit an impressive .410 in 1958, the last year the two played together. His son, Carl Jr., played shortstop and held his own with a .375 average.

Given their ages, it was only natural that when scouts came to look at the Cardinals, it was the younger Carl they were interested in. The Cincinnati Reds were aggressive, offering more money than any other team. But the younger Carl wanted to play for the Red Sox, who were closer to his home. It was probably an added bonus that, since the Sox were a team that didn't put players' names on their jerseys, he would never have to worry about wearing a uniform that had his last name, Yastrzemski, misspelled.

Who did Frank Robinson call "the most patient impatient man I've ever met"?

Earl Weaver could be a study in contrasts at time. Known for wanting quick results and quick turnarounds — Weaver was a strong believer

Modern Baseball's 30-Game Winners			
Year	Pitcher, Team	W–L	ERA
1901	Cy Young, Boston Red Sox	33–10	1.62
1902	Cy Young, Boston Red Sox	32–11	2.15
1903	Christy Mathewson, New York Giants	30–13	2.26
	Joe McGinnity, New York Giants	31–20	2.43
1904	Jack Chesbro, New York Highlanders	41–12	1.82
	Christy Mathewson, New York Giants	33–12	2.03
	Joe McGinnity, New York Giants	35–8	1.61
1905	Christy Mathewson, New York Giants	31–9	1.28
1908	Ed Walsh, Chicago White Sox	40–15	1.42
1908	Christy Mathewson, New York Giants	37–11	1.43
1910	Jack Coombs, Philadelphia Athletics	31–9	1.30
1912	Joe Wood, Boston Red Sox	34–5	1.91
	Walter Johnson, Washington Senators	33–12	1.39
1913	Walter Johnson, Washington Senators	36–7	1.14
1915	Grover Alexander, Philadelphia Phillies	31–10	1.22
1916	Grover Alexander, Philadelphia Phillies	33–12	1.55
1917	Grover Alexander, Philadelphia Phillies	30–13	1.83
1920	Jim Bagby, Cleveland Indians	31–12	2.89
1931	Lefty Grove, Philadelphia Athletics	31–4	2.06
1934	Dizzy Dean, St. Louis Cardinals	30–7	2.66
1968	Denny McLain, Detroit Tigers	31–6	1.96

in gearing an offence for big innings rather than playing smallball — he would also stick with players for a long time.

Though his approach drove fans, and sometimes players, nuts from time to time, Weaver got results. In 18 years as the Orioles manager his teams won 90 or more games 11 times, and 100 or more games five times. Only once did a Weaver squad finish below .500.

Why do some argue that Jimmie Foxx should be credited as the 1932 Triple Crown winner?

Jimmie Foxx doesn't get nearly the amount of credit that he should for the player that he was. A true great, and a power threat who challenged Babe Ruth's single-season home run record in 1932 when the Philadelphia Athletics' slugger hit 58 blasts, Foxx is oft-mentioned, but oft-forgotten when people talk about the all-time greats.

He was also a Triple Crown winner in 1933. While one Triple Crown is an incredible feat, there are those who would say that Foxx should be credited with back-to-back Triple Crowns, thanks to his incredible 1932 season. That year, Foxx, besides his near-record number of home runs, also topped the American League in RBIs with 169. He finished second in batting average to Lefty O'Doul, who batted .368. But O'Doul only had 595 at-bats that season. In 1932, that was enough to qualify for the batting crown, but in later years baseball decided that a batter had to have 3.1 at-bats for every game his team played in order to be eligible for the title. O'Doul would have fallen short, by this standard.

Who missed out on the Triple Crown by one home run in 1948?

After battling appendicitis and tonsillitis in 1947, Stan Musial of the St. Louis Cardinals bounced back with the most productive season of his career in 1948. Not only did he reach a milestone that year, collecting his 1,000th career hit, but he came within a breath of the Triple Crown.

He led the league in a number of categories — hits, doubles, triples, total bases, and slugging percentage — but it was in the big three categories that he was most impressive. Musial's .376 batting average was the league best by 43 points, and had an NL-best 131 RBIs. But while his 39 home runs were among the league's best, Musial fell a home run shy of the lead: Ralph Kiner and Johnny Mize each hit 40.

The kicker was that Musial actually did hit one more home run in a game in Philadelphia, but the game was rained out and the home run was taken off the books.

Fortunately for Stan the Man, there are other rewards besides the Triple Crown. In 1948, he became the first man to win the National League Most Valuable Player Award three times.

Which player won the hitting Triple Crown but was not named league Most Valuable Player?

Red Sox fans are still seething over the snub of Ted Williams in 1942. Williams batted .356 with 36 home runs and 137 RBIs that year, leading the American League in all three categories. But when the votes for Most Valuable Player were tabulated, Williams finished second. To add to the sting, he finished second to a Yankee: Joe Gordon. Gordon posted a .322 average with 18 home runs and 103 RBIs — good numbers, but he was greatly outclassed by Williams at the plate. In fact, the only offensive categories Gordon led the league in were strikeouts and double-play groundouts. Gordon's defence was seen as enough to make him more valuable than Williams.

Since the MVP award has been established, Williams is the only man to win the Triple Crown but not the MVP.

Switch-Hitters Who Have Led Their League in RBIs		
Player, Team	Season	RBIs
Mickey Mantle, New York Yankees	1956	130
Eddie Murray, Baltimore Orioles	1981	78
Ruben Sierra, Texas Rangers	1989	119
Howard Johnson, New York Mets	1991	117
Lance Berkman, Houston Astros	2002	128

Who is featured on the world's most valuable baseball card?

The most valuable baseball card in history was issued in 1909 and features Honus Wagner. One in mint condition sold for $110,000 in 1988. The reason it became so valuable is its scarcity — it was issued by the Sweet Caporal Cigarette Company, but Wagner, an eight-time National League batting champion, had it discontinued because he didn't want to promote smoking among children.

Who was the first major league player to have his number retired?

Nicknamed "The Iron Horse" because of the durability that enabled him to play a then-record 2,130 consecutive games, Lou Gehrig's career was cut short when he was diagnosed with Amyotrophic Lateral Sclerosis (ALS, which is now commonly known as Lou Gehrig's Disease). The Yankees honoured their departing hero on July 4, 1939, with a pre-game ceremony. That day the Yankees made Gehrig's number 4 permanently unavailable to any other player. It was the first time a major league baseball player's number was retired.

What number has been retired by every Major League Baseball team and why?

In 1997, 50 years after he broke the colour barrier, every Major League Baseball team retired Jackie Robinson's number 42. Active players who had the number before 1997 are allowed to wear it until they retire, but after that the number will never be worn again. Two who kept wearing number 42 are Mo Vaughn and Butch Huskey, both of whom chose the number as a tribute to Robinson.

How many times did Reggie Jackson win the home run crown outright?

The self-proclaimed "Straw That Stirs the Drink" had a legendary career as a member of the Athletics, Yankees, Orioles, and Angels, and was noted for his power, amassing a career 563 dingers. Along the way, Jackson led the league in home runs four times — but only once did he win the crown outright, when he hit 32 homers in 1973.

Five Hall of Fame Pitchers Who Never Won the Cy Young Award*
- Rich Gossage
- Juan Marichal
- Phil Niekro
- Nolan Ryan
- Don Sutton

*Since 1956, when the Cy Young Award was introduced.

The other three times Jackson tied another player. Coincidentally, on each of those occasions he was matched by a member of the Milwaukee Brewers. George Scott matched Reggie's 36 swats in 1975, Ben Oglivie hit 41 in 1980, and Gorman Thomas hit 39 in 1982.

None of those were Jackson's biggest home run year. In 1969 he clubbed 47 round-trippers, only to be bested by the Twins' Harmon Killebrew, who hit 49.

Who had a career batting average of .356, but never won a batting title?

In most years, especially nowadays, a .356 average over the course of a single season would be enough to win a batting crown. But Shoeless Joe Jackson compiled that average over the course of a career — the third highest career batting average in the history of the game. Along the way he batted over .380 four times.

And yet, not once did he have a league-leading batting average. The closest he came was in 1911. That year Jackson had what still holds up as the 15th highest single season batting average in major league history when he hit .408. That same year Ty Cobb batted .419.

Which pitcher lost no-hit bids with two outs in the ninth in back-to-back starts in 1988?

Dave Stieb of the Toronto Blue Jays was the poster-child for no-hitter heartbreak. Five times he had no-hit bids spoiled, and the most agonizing examples were back-to-back starts in 1988. On September 23, Stieb was one out away from a no-hitter against the Cleveland Indians when a bad hop on a grounder by Julio Franco spoiled the bid. In Stieb's next start, Jim Traber of the Baltimore Orioles crushed the hopes of Toronto fans when he singled to right on a 2–2 pitch with two outs in the ninth.

The next season Stieb lost a perfect game with two outs in the ninth. It wasn't until September 2, 1990, that Stieb finally joined the no-hitter club.

Which 300-game winner had the fewest shutouts?

In the era of the five-man rotation, starters had fewer opportunities to earn wins, making it more difficult to reach the 300-win plateau. During the late 1980s, many were speculating that we might never see a new

Pitchers Who Have Won the Cy Young Award and MVP in the Same Season		
Player	Team	Year
Don Newcombe	Brooklyn Dodgers	1956
Sandy Koufax	Los Angeles Dodgers	1963
Denny McLain	Detroit Tigers	1968
Bob Gibson	St. Louis Cardinals	1968
Vida Blue	Oakland Athletics	1971
Rollie Fingers	Milwaukee Brewers	1981
Willie Hernandez	Detroit Tigers	1984
Roger Clemens	Boston Red Sox	1986
Dennis Eckersley	Oakland Athletics	1992

pitcher emerge who would have a 300-win career. But Tom Glavine's arrival in Atlanta not only helped the Braves to become a perennial contender, it proved that even in the modern game pitchers could rack up wins and pass the three-century mark.

But Glavine not only pitched in an era with fewer win opportunities — he also pitched in an era of explosive offences, and he has the fewest career shutouts (25) of any pitcher in the 300-win club.

Which two hitters have led their leagues in strikeouts and batting average in the same season?

Babe Ruth seemed to put up big numbers in every category. He set records for home runs and walks, but he also set records for strikeouts. No one seemed to mind the K totals, but they did help to earn a somewhat dubious place in baseball history in 1924, when he became the first player to lead his league in strikeouts (81) and batting average .378. Jimmie Foxx wouldn't leave Ruth alone in that club for long — nine years later, in 1933, his 93 strikeouts and .356 batting average were tops in the league.

Incidentally, both players also contributed their share of home runs in those seasons, with 46 and 48 respectively.

Where did Babe Ruth hit his first professional home run?

In 1914 Babe Ruth was still in the minor leagues, playing with the AAA Providence Grays. On September 5, the Grays played an away game against the Toronto Maple Leafs at Hanlan's Point on Toronto Island. It was here that Babe Ruth hit his first professional home run, and the only home run of his minor league career as he was recruited into the major leagues the next season. Hanlan's Point is now considered a historic site and there are three commemorative plaques marking the first home run of the Bambino's career.

Which pitcher won only 131 major league games, but was a two-time Cy Young Award winner?

Some pitchers dominate for years, some are inconsistent, and some have brief periods of brilliance before flaming out. Denny McLain fell into the latter category. McClain seemed destined for greatness, perhaps even the Hall of Fame, when he exploded onto the baseball scene. He won 17 games in 1967, then overwhelmed the American League with 31 wins and a 1.96 ERA in 1968 as he became the last pitcher to win 31 games in a season. He was named the Cy Young Award winner that year.

The following season, McLain backed up his amazing 1968 with 24 wins, a 2.80 ERA, and another Cy Young Award.

And that was it. As quickly as McLain jumped out of the gates, he disappeared just as quickly. Gambling problems and other off-field activities led to suspensions, a suspicious foot injury (*Sports Illustrated* reported that the foot was damaged as punishment for a gambling debt), and inconsistent performances on the field. By 1973, McLain was finished in baseball.

Baseball's All-Century Team*	
Player	Position
Nolan Ryan	Pitcher
Sandy Koufax	Pitcher
Cy Young	Pitcher
Roger Clemens	Pitcher
Bob Gibson	Pitcher
Walter Johnson	Pitcher
Warren Spahn	Pitcher
Christy Mathewson	Pitcher
Lefty Grove	Pitcher
Johnny Bench	Catcher
Yogi Berra	Catcher
Lou Gehrig	First Base
Mark McGwire	First Base
Jackie Robinson	Second Base
Rogers Hornsby	Second Base
Mike Schmidt	Third Base
Brooks Robinson	Third Base
Cal Ripken Jr.	Shortstop
Ernie Banks	Shortstop
Honus Wagner	Shortstop
Babe Ruth	Outfield
Henry Aaron	Outfield
Ted Williams	Outfield
Willie Mays	Outfield
Joe DiMaggio	Outfield
Mickey Mantle	Outfield
Ty Cobb	Outfield
Ken Griffey Jr.	Outfield
Pete Rose	Outfield
Stan Musial	Outfield

*As selected by online votes in a 1999 poll by Major League Baseball.

traditions
and superstitions

When did it become customary to play national anthems at major league games?

By September 1918, the United States had joined World War I and there was a patriotic fervour that was felt in all aspects of American life, particularly all-American activities such as baseball. During the seventh-inning stretch of Game 1 of the World Series at Chicago's Comiskey Park, the stadium band began playing "The Star Spangled Banner." Though the song was not the official U.S. anthem yet (it achieved that status in 1931), it stirred the hearts of a nation at war. From then on the song became a tradition at games, and by World War II was played before every contest.

> **They Said It ...**
> "Sometimes when you're driving, the car just seems to turn by itself into a McDonald's, and while you're there, you might as well get a large order of fries."
> *Boog Powell.*

What did Julio Gotay keep in his back pocket during games?

Superstition and professional sports seem to go hand in hand, and baseball is no exception. Many players have taboos and rituals before, during, and after games. Some refuse to shave on game day, some avoid stepping on the foul line when taking the field. Some players are notorious for their superstitions: Wade Boggs, for example, had a number of rituals, such as leaving his house at the exact same time for every game and eating chicken before each game.

But Boggs was a superstar. When you're Julio Gotay, your ritual has to be something special in order for you to be remembered, and Gotay's ritual was, indeed, unique. He kept a cheese sandwich in his back pocket for every game. It must have done some good — he managed to last 10 seasons and played with four different teams.

What do the Hanshin Tigers have to do to win the Japan Championship Series?

When the Hanshin Tigers knocked off the Seibu Lions to win the Japan Championship Series in 1985, their fans were understandably enthused. But celebrations got a little out of control. One large group of celebrants marked the win by jumping from the Ebisubashi Bridge into the canal below. When the rowdy lot ran out of willing jumpers, they turned their attentions to a statue of Colonel Sanders in front of a nearby Kentucky Fried Chicken. The Colonel was tossed into the canal, where it has rested ever since.

The Tigers have not won a Japan Championship Series since, and it has been said that the angry Colonel cursed the team. They will not be able to win the championship again until he is rescued from the canal's bottom and returned to his original location.

Sadly, the easy solution — recovering the statue — has proven to be anything but easy. Multiple searches for the Colonel have proven fruitless.

They Said It ...
"They couldn't break a chandelier if they held batting practice in a hotel lobby."
Red Sox pitcher Bill Lee on the California Angels' hitters.

When did teams start allowing fans to keep balls hit into the stands?

Ironically, it was the Chicago Cubs — whose fans would later become known for throwing back home run balls hit by opponents — who first decided that balls hit into the stands were up for grabs.

In the early 1900s, fans were expected to return any ball they caught. Those who tried to keep the balls as souvenirs were confronted by security guards, resulting in frequent scuffles and occasional arrests. Charles Weeghman, owner of the Cubs, grew tired of these incidents and allowed fans to keep any ball hit their way.

However, the idea didn't catch on right away. In the 1930s a ball was caught in the mesh behind home plate at Yankee Stadium. A fan grabbed the ball and was beaten by ushers. He sued the team, and was awarded

130

$7,500 in compensation. Baseball then allowed fans league-wide to keep souvenir balls without having to face the wrath of stadium employees.

> **They Said It …**
> "I can't hit the ball until I hit the bottle."
> *Pete Browning, 19th-century slugger.*

Why don't baseball coaches wear civilian clothes like those in every other sport?

In the 1800s, baseball managers looked after travel and logistics, while a uniformed playing captain guided the team on the field. Captains who had retired from playing kept their uniforms on in case they were needed as a player. Eventually the manager's job expanded to include coaching, but tradition and a 1957 rule insisted that no one without a uniform could enter the playing area, including base coaches and the managers.

During the early 20th century, the legendary Connie Mack managed the Philadelphia Athletics while wearing a suit and tie, but he never left the dugout.

Which five teams do not put the name of their city or region on their road uniforms?

Traditionally, teams proudly display the name of the city or region they represent on their road uniforms. In fact, for many years in the early days of baseball, nearly every team put their city or region name on their home *and* road uniforms.

Though uniform changes for one or more teams occur almost every year, currently there are five teams that do not honour their city or region on their road attire: the Los Angeles Angels of Anaheim, the Milwaukee Brewers, the Philadelphia Phillies, the St. Louis Cardinals, and the Tampa Bay Rays.

> **Quickies**
> *Did you know …*
> • that Ben Oglivie, who tied Reggie Jackson for the home run crown in 1980 with 41, weighed only 170 pounds? The only other player that small to hit that many home runs was Mel Ott, who hit 42 home runs in 1929.

Why did baseball players begin wearing knickers?

Originally, baseball teams wore regular pants as part of their uniforms. But in 1867, the wife of the owner of Cincinnati's team came up with the idea of giving the players red socks to wear. To show off the socks, the team opted for the shorter knickers, and became known as the Cincinnati Red Stockings.

Why is a ball to the face of a 16-year-old credited with breaking the Curse of the Bambino?

If Babe Ruth really did curse the Boston Red Sox when they sold him to the Yankees, then perhaps Manny Ramirez ended that curse, in a bloody way, on September 2, 2004. The Red Sox were leading the Anaheim Angels by two runs when Manny hit a ball into the seats on the foul side of Pesky Pole. It would have been just another long, loud strike, except that it struck 16-year-old Lee Gavin in the face, splitting his lip and knocking out two teeth.

It was tough luck for the kid, but some Curse theorists saw greater significance. Gavin had lived his entire life in an old farmhouse on Dutton Road in Sudbury, Massachusetts. The dwelling is known as Home Plate Farm — a name given to it by its former owner ... Babe Ruth.

They Said It ...
"Just to have his body, I'd trade mine and my wife's and throw in some cash."
Pete Rose on Mike Schmidt.

The Red Sox won the game, 10–7. That same evening, the Yankees were throttled 22–0 by the Cleveland Indians. Some said that this was a sure sign that the Curse was broken the moment Lee Gavin's face was broken. As it turned out, the Red Sox went on to win the World Series.

Which baseball legend is 6'6", weighs 300 pounds, and was born on the Galapagos Islands?

According to his official profile in the Philadelphia Phillies media guide, the Phillie Phanatic is the legend in question. His profile also notes that, among other things, he suffers from a slight case of body odour.

The Phanatic is considered one of the great sports mascots. He's entertained Phillies fans since 1978.

Which actress, best known for her work on TV's *Friends*, began helping the Anaheim Angels win games in 2000?

The Anaheim Angels began using a clip of a monkey from the film *Ace Ventura: Pet Detective* to inspire the team in close, late-inning contests in 2000. Somehow, the tactic worked, and quickly the "Rally Monkey" became a phenomenon. The *Ace Ventura* footage was soon replaced, as the Angels wanted to hire a full-time monkey to be the motivational clipster. They inked Katie, a monkey who had made several appearances on *Friends* as Ross Geller's pet, to be the official Rally Monkey. Two years later, the Rally Monkey helped lead the Angels to their first World Series win.

> **They Said It ...**
> "Pete Rose is the best thing to happen to the game since, well, the game."
> *Sparky Anderson.*

the
best
of the
best:
baseball's
thirty most
memorable
moments

1. Jackie Robinson's First Game — April 15, 1947

Baseball changed forever when Jackie Robinson became the first African-American to play in the major leagues in the modern era. It was the one moment in the game's history that was bigger than the sport itself. Years before the Civil Rights Movement, Robinson was a force for change, and his impact extended beyond that first game. Robinson faced horrible racism during the early part of his career, but his even temperament made it possible for other Black players to follow him to the big leagues.

2. Bobby Thomson's Home Run — October 3, 1951

It took more than one game to make Bobby Thomson's home run legendary. The Brooklyn Dodgers had led the National League by 13½ games in mid-August of 1951, but while the Dodgers played steady ball the rest of the way, the New York Giants went on a tear, winning 37 of their final 44 games. At season's end, the two teams were in a dead heat, and a three-game playoff was held to decide the pennant. The teams split the first two games. Then, in the bottom of the ninth in Game 3, the Giants trailed 4–2 with one out when Bobby Thomson came to the plate. Dodger reliever Ralph Branca, wearing number 13, threw two fastballs. Thomson watched the first, then teed off on the second, smoking a line drive into the lower deck in left field at the Polo Grounds to send the Giants to the World Series. It was one of many heartbreaks for the Dodgers in the "Boys of Summer" era.

> **Quickies**
> *Did you know ...*
> * that during the 1951 tiebreaker playoff against the Brooklyn Dodgers, the New York Giants were stealing signs? A man in the outfield stands was relaying the catchers' signals to Giants players, though Bobby Thomson maintains he was not given a sign when he hit his home run.

3. Joe Carter Touches 'Em All — October 23, 1993

The Toronto Blue Jays were defending World Series Champions and were leading the 1993 World Series 3–2, but in Game 6 they had their backs to the wall and it looked as though there would be a Game 7. But after Philadelphia Phillies closer Mitch Williams walked Rickey Henderson and surrendered a hit to Paul Molitor, the stage was set for Joe Carter. After two balls, Williams came back to even the count at 2–2. Carter, who had seen Williams struggling with every other pitch, was looking for a slider, and that's what he got. He hit a three-run homer into the left field bullpen to give Toronto an 8–6 win and a World Championship. It was only the second time a World Series had ended on a home run, and the first time one had ended on a come-from-behind, game-winning blast.

4. "I Don't Believe What I Just Saw!" — October 15, 1988

Kirk Gibson had been the heart of the Los Angeles Dodgers all season long in 1988, leading them to a National League Championship; but by the time the World Series got underway, he was suffering from injuries to both legs. He wasn't expected to play in the series, but manager Tommy Lasorda kept him on the roster "just in case." In Game 1, the Dodgers trailed the Oakland Athletics 4–3 with two outs in the ninth. They had a man on second and Alejandro Pena scheduled to bat until Lasorda pulled him back and Gibson limped out of the dugout toward the plate.

After feeble swings on the first two pitches, Gibson fought back to bring the count full. Gibson was counting on A's closer Dennis Eckersley to throw a backdoor slider, and that's what he did. Gibson hit a home run to right field, and hobbled around the bases to complete the improbable heroic act. It was his only at-bat in the series, which the Dodgers swept. Jack Buck was calling that game, and fans always go back to the sound bite of him yelling, "I don't believe what I just saw!"

5. Carlton Fisk Ends the Marathon — October 21, 1975

Many still consider it the greatest game ever played. The Boston Red Sox came in to Game 6 of the 1975 World Series trailing three games to two. The back and forth affair had each team overcoming three-run deficits, and at the end of nine innings the game remained tied. Finally, in the bottom of the 12th, Carlton Fisk hit a high shot toward left field that just barely stayed fair and cleared the Green Monster. While the Red Sox ended up losing the Series the following day, Fisk's heroic blast is one of the most cherished sports memories in New England.

> **Quickies**
> *Did you know ...*
> • that the pitch Kirk Gibson hit for a home run in the 1988 World Series was predicted by a Dodger scout? Mel Didier had said that given a 3–2 count in a pressure situation against a left-handed batter, closer Dennis Eckersley would come in with a backdoor slider every single time.

6. Bucky Dent Breaks the Red Sox's Hearts — October 2, 1978

The Red Sox appeared to be cruising to a division title in 1978, leading by 14½ games in July. From that point on, the Red Sox floundered while the Yankees surged, ending the season with a 39–14 stretch, including a four-game sweep of the Sox in September. The teams were tied at season's end, and the rivals met in a one-game tiebreaker at Fenway Park. The game was close, with the Red Sox up 2–0 until Yankee shortstop Bucky Dent came up in the top of the seventh and hit a three-run home run that sunk the Red Sox and completed the Yankees' 1978 comeback.

7. Dave Stieb: "Today I'll Be Perfect" — September 2, 1990

There was no greater story of heartbreak in the 1980s and 1990s than Dave Stieb. One of the best pitchers of his era, Stieb had narrowly missed no-hitters on five occasions. The most gut-wrenching, lost no-hitter seemed to occur on September 24, 1988, when, with two outs in the ninth inning, Julio Franco of the Cleveland Indians hit a bouncer that took a bad hop to break Stieb's heart. Then, in Stieb's very next start on September 30, he took a no-hitter into the ninth again, and, with two outs, watched in agony as Jim Traber singled to break up a second straight no-hit bid. These crushers made fans wonder if the title of Stieb's autobiography, *Tomorrow I'll Be Perfect*, would ever be anything more than wishful thinking. Finally, on September 2, 1990, he was perfect — or close to it. Stieb took a no-hitter to the ninth one last time and, with two outs, Jerry Browne hit a scorcher to right field — right at outfielder Junior Felix, who made the final out.

8. Nolan Ryan's Seventh No-Hitter — May 1, 1991

Nolan Ryan was known for three things: his blazing fastball, his high strikeout totals, and his no-hitters. When he pitched his fifth no-hitter in 1981, many thought he'd reached the highest heights he'd ever reach, breaking the record of Sandy Koufax. But in 1991, as he stared down Roberto Alomar of the Toronto Blue Jays with two outs in the bottom of the ninth, he was on the verge of an inhuman seventh no-hitter. Alomar himself was in the early years of one of the great second-base careers of the era, but was no match for the Ryan Express, striking out to end the game.

9. Roger Maris Out-Slugs the Babe — October 1, 1961

For much of the season it was a two-horse race. Yankee teammates Roger Maris and Mickey Mantle were matching each other blow-for-blow as they set sights on Babe Ruth's single-season home run record. But Mantle tailed off, while Maris kept up his torrid pace. With media pressure at levels rarely seen before, Maris's 1961 became one of the most stressful on record. His hair was falling out in clumps, and at one point he asked his manager if it would make him any less of a man to bunt if it would help his team win. But Maris ended up swinging away anyway, and on the last day of the season he hit his 61st home run into the right field stands at Yankee Stadium.

10. Mazeroski's Home Run — October 13, 1960

The Pittsburgh Pirates were heavy underdogs in the 1960 World Series against the New York Yankees, and it seemed like a miracle in itself that they were able to make it to Game 7. Even then, it appeared to be the most one-sided tie series ever played, with the Yankees dominating in their wins while the Pirates barely eked out their victories. But World Series aren't won on aggregate, and when Game 7 went to the bottom of the ninth inning with the score still tied, Bill Mazeroski stroked a solo home run to win the game and the series. It was the first time a World Series had ended with a home run, and remains the only time a Game 7 has ended with a home run.

11. Henry "Hank" Aaron Breaks the Unbreakable Record — April 8, 1974

The pressure of chasing a Babe Ruth home run record would be enormous for anyone — there were many people who wanted Ruth's records to stand forever. Roger Maris felt the pressure in 1961, but Hank Aaron was under more pressure than any athlete should endure. He was not just a modern-day player pursuing the Babe — he was a black player, and for an element of society, that was unpardonable. Aaron faced death threats that were overtly racist. Hammerin' Hank overcame the threats and the pressures, and on April 8 he hit his record-breaking 715th home run in front of the hometown crowd at Atlanta's Fulton County Stadium.

12. Cal Ripken Passes Lou Gehrig — September 6, 1995

The 1994 Major League Baseball players' strike was nearly catastrophic, so the sport was looking for a "good news" story. They didn't have to look far — they only had to look to a story that people had already been following for years. Cal Ripken had not missed a baseball game since May 30, 1982, and was on the verge of breaking Lou Gehrig's record playing streak — a record that many had once thought unbreakable. On September 6, 1995, at Camden Yards in Baltimore, the hometown hero played his 2,131st straight game.

13. Barry Bonds Hits Number 756 — August 7, 2007

The label "colourful and controversial" never suited any athlete the way it suited Barry Bonds. The outspoken outfielder was revered for his talent, but was rumoured to be enhancing that talent with steroids. On August 7, 2007, that didn't matter to San Francisco Giants fans, who were elated to see their hero hit his 756th home run, breaking the record of Hank Aaron.

Quickies

Did you know ...

- that when Barry Bonds hit a record 73 home runs in 2001, it was 24 home runs more than his highest total in any other season of his career?

14. Mark McGwire Passes Maris — September 8, 1998

A phenomenal battle between Mark McGwire and Sammy Sosa marked 1998, as they put up home run numbers that had never been seen before. McGwire had hit 58 home runs the previous season and all eyes were on him as he came into the year prepared to make an assault on Roger Maris's record. Sammy Sosa surprised most by joining that assault. But Mark McGwire was the first to catch Maris, hitting his 62nd home run on September 8. Sosa would catch up to McGwire, and on September 25 slugged his 66th home run, taking temporary possession of the record. McGwire retook the lead, hitting five home runs in the final series of the season, and finished the year with 70 longballs.

15. The Boston Red Sox Reverse the Curse — 2004

Boston fans had their share of heartbreaks over the years, and often the heartbreaks were at the hands of the New York Yankees. It was fitting, then, that the Red Sox' greatest postseason miracle came against their rivals. In 2004, the Yankees took a 3–0 series lead in the American League Championship Series, and it looked certain that the Red Sox would, once again, go down in defeat. But the Red Sox won the next four games, becoming the first team in baseball history to overcome a 3–0 deficit to win a postseason series. The World Series was anticlimactic, with the Sox sweeping the St. Louis Cardinals to win their first title since 1918.

> **They Said It …**
>
> "Smith corks one into right down the line … it may go … Go crazy, folks, go crazy! It's a home run! And the Cardinals have won the game 3–2 on a home run by the Wizard! Go crazy, folks, go crazy!"
> *Jack Buck calling Ozzie Smith's home run to win Game 5 of the 1985 National League Championship Series.*

16. Buckner's Error — October 25, 1986

The greatest heartbreak in Red Sox history was also one of the most thrilling moments in New York Mets history. In 1986, the Red Sox were on the verge of erasing years of heartbreak by winning the World Series. Up three games to two, the Red Sox took a 5–3 lead to the bottom of the ninth. After two quick outs, victory seemed assured. Then the ceiling caved in. Relievers Calvin Schiraldi and Bob Stanley couldn't get batters out, and the Mets rallied for two runs to tie the game. Then, with two outs and Ray Knight on second, Mookie Wilson hit an easy groundball down the first base line. Bill Buckner inexplicably misplayed the ball, allowing it to go between his legs, Knight scored, and the next day, the Mets won Game 7.

17. Lou Gehrig Day — July 4, 1939

Lou Gehrig had been a Yankee hero since his first full season in 1925, and fans were stunned when they learned that he had been diagnosed with

Amyotrophic Lateral Sclerosis (ALS). With his life slipping away, Gehrig was honoured with a tribute at Yankee Stadium in which he became the first player in baseball to have his number retired. At the ceremony, Gehrig delivered one of the most famous lines ever spoken: "Today I consider myself the luckiest man on the face of the earth." Gehrig died less than two years later. The disease that took his life has been more commonly known as Lou Gehrig's disease ever since.

18. "Did DiMaggio Get a Hit Today?" — 1941

That was the question virtually everyone in the baseball world was asking in May, June, and July of 1941 as they checked the daily scores from the major leagues. DiMaggio's hit streak captured a nation, and when he hit safely in his 46th consecutive game, he broke Willie Keeler's 1897 record. And then DiMaggio continued to get a hit every day for nearly two more weeks. Finally, two outstanding defensive plays by the Cleveland Indians ended the streak at 56 games. No one has even come close since, with the longest post-DiMaggio streak at "only" 44 games.

> **Quickies**
> *Did you know ...*
> • that after Joe DiMaggio's 56-game hitting streak ended in 1941, he went on another streak of 16 games? In total, DiMaggio hit safely in 72 of 73 games.

19. Ted Williams Bats .406 — 1941

In the late 19th and early 20th centuries, .400 batting averages were more commonplace than they would later become. By 1941, they were a rarity, so all eyes were on Ted Williams of the Boston Red Sox as he spent much of the year above the magic number. On the last day of the season the Sox were playing a doubleheader; Williams' average sat at .39955 — which would round up to .400. Red Sox manager Joe Cronin offered to let Williams sit out the doubleheader. Williams insisted on playing, and went six for eight to finish the season with a .406 average. No player has finished higher than .390 since.

20. The Bums Finally Win One — October 4, 1955

The 1940s and 1950s were a special time for fans of the Brooklyn Dodgers. The team had made history by signing Jackie Robinson, and they continued to stay in the headlines by winning or contending every year. But as much as they won, they couldn't win it all. There were gut-wrenching defeats that prevented them from going to the World Series, and when they did get to the big stage, they lost. Between 1947 and 1953, the Dodgers made the Series four times, losing to the Yankees on each occasion. But in 1955, thanks to a tremendous Game 7 by starting pitcher Johnny Podres and an outstanding catch by Junior Gilliam on a drive destined for extra bases, the Dodgers finally beat the Yankees and won their first, and only, World Series in Brooklyn.

21. The Perfect Game — October 8, 1956

He wasn't the team's top pitcher, and after a subpar performance in Game 2 of the 1956 World Series, Don Larsen didn't know if he'd even get a chance to start again. But manager Casey Stengel gave him the game ball for Game 5, and Larsen made his skipper look good. Against a fearsome Brooklyn Dodgers lineup that included the likes of Duke Snider, Roy Campanella, and Jackie Robinson, Larsen was perfect. After retiring the first 26 batters in order, he struck out pinch-hitter Dale Mitchell to become the first — and to date, the only — pitcher to throw a no-hitter or perfect game in postseason play.

> **Quickies**
> *Did you know ...*
> - that Don Larsen had an unusual windup ... in that he had virtually no windup? Larsen pitched from the stretch regardless of whether the bases were occupied or not.

22. Roberto Clemente's 3,000th Hit — September 30, 1972

Some moments are great when they happen, and the greatness fades over time; but Roberto Clemente's 3,000th hit was a moment that became greater in the following weeks. In the waning days of the 1972 season, Clemente singled to join the exclusive 3,000 hit club. Three months later, on New Year's Eve, he got on a plane on a humanitarian mission to help earthquake victims in Nicaragua. The plane never reached its destination as it went down, killing Clemente and all aboard.

23. The Pine Tar Incident — July 24, 1983

The controversy would have been newsworthy regardless of how George Brett reacted, but the enduring fame of The Pine Tar Incident is undoubtedly due to the famous footage of Brett's charge from the dugout.

With his Kansas City Royals trailing 4–3 with two out in the ninth, Brett hit what he thought was a two-run home run to give the Royals the lead. But Yankees manager Billy Martin had been keeping an eye on Brett's bat for some time, waiting for the opportune moment to point out to the umpires that the pine tar Brett used to help grip the bat extended further up the barrel than league regulations allowed. The umpire, Tim McClelland, called Brett out, ending the game, and Brett charged the umpire and needed to be restrained by teammates and coaches.

After an appeal to the league, the umpire's call was overruled, Brett's home run was allowed to stand, and the two teams met on August 18 to finish the ninth inning of a Royals victory.

24. Ted Williams Goes Out with a Blast — September 28, 1960

Ted Williams was one of the greatest offensive players the game has ever known, and his lifetime batting average of .344 is a testament to that fact. He also hit 521 home runs in his career — none more memorable than the last. Williams had already announced his retirement, so when he came to the plate in the eighth inning on the last day of the season, everyone knew it would be his last plate appearance. Fans would have forgiven him for a mere single, or even an out, but Williams finished his career with a home run.

25. The Improbable Comeback — October 20, 1993

One of the wildest games in World Series history took place in Game 4 of the 1993 battle between the Toronto Blue Jays and the Philadelphia Phillies. Philadelphia's Lenny Dykstra narrowly missed a record-tying third home run in the game, Jays starter Todd Stottlemyre nearly knocked himself unconscious with the least graceful slide into third in living memory, and run after run was being put on the board. It would be generous to the Jays to say the game was a see-saw battle — though they staged mini-comebacks at times, the Phillies seemed to be in control, and by the eighth inning had a 14–9 lead. But Mitch Williams, the Phillies' closer, couldn't get Jays batters out. With four runs already in, Devon White hit a looper to right-centre that bounced in and went to the wall. Two runs plated, and the Jays hung on to win, 15–14.

26. Rose's 4,192 — September 11, 1985

Before the gambling controversy, Pete Rose was one of the most beloved figures in the game, particularly in Cincinnati, where he spent most of his career. In 1985, as the Reds' player-manager, Rose was staring down a record he'd been pursuing his entire career: Ty Cobb's hit record of 4,191. By September 10, he'd tied Cobb and needed one more hit to own the record outright. Television networks — in the days before round-the-clock sports coverage — made the rare decision to cut into regular programming to bring live coverage of each of Rose's at-bats. Rose singled up the middle to pass Cobb.

27. Three Pitches, Three Swings, Three Home Runs — October 18, 1977

The 1977 World Series was the first between the New York Yankees and Los Angeles Dodgers since 1963, and renewed one of the most storied rivalries in the game. But Reggie Jackson stole the show in Game 6 with one of the most impressive power displays in postseason history. Not only did Jackson tie Babe Ruth's record with three home runs in a game, but he did so on three straight pitches. The victims were Burt Hooton (fourth inning), Elias Sosa (fifth inning), and Charlie Hough (eighth inning).

28. Blue Monday — October 19, 1981

Montreal Expos fans took a few shots to the gut during the team's all-too-brief history. The Expos' fantastic 1994 season was wiped out by a players' strike; then, after years of management and attendance troubles, the team was moved to Washington, D.C. But the most agonizing moment may have been Blue Monday. The Expos were playing in their first National League Championship Series and were in a tight duel with the Los Angeles Dodgers in the decisive Game 5, tied at 1–1 in the ninth. With their star pitcher, Steve Rogers, working in relief, the Expos seemed to be in good shape, until Rick Monday hit a home run to right field that gave the Dodgers the lead and, a half-inning later, the series win.

29. Johnny Vander Meer — June 11–15, 1938

For some, a no-hitter is a career achievement. For others, like Sandy Koufax and Nolan Ryan, no-hitters are slightly easier to come by, though still rare. But even Ryan and Koufax never pulled off a feat like that of the Cincinnati Reds' Johnny Vander Meer in 1938. A decent pitcher who would go 15–10 that year, Vander Meer nevertheless never seemed headed for greatness. And even when he no-hit the Boston Braves on June 11, 1938, he was just one of many pitchers with no-hitters to their credit. But in his next start he made history by pitching his second consecutive no-hitter, this time against the Brooklyn Dodgers.

30. The Catch — September 29, 1954

There have been greater catches, and perhaps even greater catches in the World Series, but when Willie Mays of the New York Giants made his famous over-the-shoulder catch in the 1954 World Series, there was more to it than the catch alone. With two men on and the score tied 2–2 in the eighth inning of Game 1, Vic Wertz hit a line drive over his head and Mays had a long, long way to run. He ended up catching the ball on the warning track, 460 feet from home plate, then whirled and threw the ball to the infield. The runners had been moving, thinking the ball was unreachable, and had to scramble back to their bases. Ultimately, the side was retired and the Giants won the game in the tenth.

champions
and award winners

World Series Results

Year	Winners	Finalists	Result
1903	Boston Americans	Pittsburgh Pirates	5–3
1904	No series		
1905	New York Giants	Philadelphia Athletics	4–1
1906	Chicago White Sox	Chicago Cubs	4–2
1907	Chicago Cubs	Detroit Tigers	4–0
1908	Chicago Cubs	Detroit Tigers	4–1
1909	Pittsburgh Pirates	Detroit Tigers	4–3
1910	Philadelphia Athletics	Chicago Cubs	4–1
1911	Philadelphia Athletics	New York Giants	4–2
1912	Boston Red Sox	New York Giants	4–3
1913	Philadelphia Athletics	New York Giants	4–1
1914	Boston Braves	Philadelphia Athletics	4–0
1915	Boston Red Sox	Philadelphia Phillies	4–1
1916	Boston Red Sox	Brooklyn Robins	4–1
1917	Chicago White Sox	New York Giants	4–2
1918	Boston Red Sox	Chicago Cubs	4–2
1919	Cincinnati Reds	Chicago White Sox	5–3
1920	Cleveland Indians	Brooklyn Robins	5–2
1921	New York Giants	New York Yankees	5–3
1922	New York Giants	New York Yankees	4–0
1923	New York Yankees	New York Giants	4–2
1924	Washington Senators	New York Giants	4–3
1925	Pittsburgh Pirates	Washington Senators	4–3
1926	St. Louis Cardinals	New York Yankees	4–3
1927	New York Yankees	Pittsburgh Pirates	4–0
1928	New York Yankees	St. Louis Cardinals	4–0
1929	Philadelphia Athletics	Chicago Cubs	4–1
1930	Philadelphia Athletics	St. Louis Cardinals	4–2
1931	St. Louis Cardinals	Philadelphia Athletics	4–3
1932	New York Yankees	Chicago Cubs	4–0

1933	New York Giants	Washington Senators	4–1
1934	St. Louis Cardinals	Detroit	4–3
1935	Detroit Tigers	Chicago Cubs	4–2
1936	New York Yankees	New York Giants	4–2
1937	New York Yankees	New York Giants	4–1
1938	New York Yankees	Chicago Cubs	4–0
1939	New York Yankees	Cincinnati Reds	4–0
1940	Cincinnati Reds	Detroit Tigers	4–3
1941	New York Yankees	Brooklyn Dodgers	4–1
1942	St. Louis Cardinals	New York Yankees	4–1
1943	New York Yankees	St. Louis Cardinals	4–1
1944	St. Louis Cardinals	St. Louis Browns	4–2
1945	Detroit Tigers	Chicago Cubs	4–3
1946	St. Louis Cardinals	Boston Red Sox	4–3
1947	New York Yankees	Brooklyn Dodgers	4–3
1948	Cleveland Indians	Boston Braves	4–2
1949	New York Yankees	Brooklyn Dodgers	4–1
1950	New York Yankees	Philadelphia Phillies	4–0
1951	New York Yankees	New York Giants	4–2
1952	New York Yankees	Brooklyn Dodgers	4–3
1953	New York Yankees	Brooklyn Dodgers	4–2
1954	New York Giants	Cleveland Indians	4–0
1955	Brooklyn Dodgers	New York Yankees	4–3
1956	New York Yankees	Brooklyn Dodgers	4–3
1957	Milwaukee Braves	New York Yankees	4–3
1958	New York Yankees	Milwaukee Braves	4–3
1959	Los Angeles Dodgers	Chicago White Sox	4–2
1960	Pittsburgh Pirates	New York Yankees	4–3
1961	New York Yankees	Cincinnati Reds	4–1
1962	New York Yankees	San Francisco Giants	4–3
1963	Los Angeles Dodgers	New York Yankees	4–0
1964	St. Louis Cardinals	New York Yankees	4–3
1965	Los Angeles Dodgers	Minnesota Twins	4–3

1966	Baltimore Orioles	Los Angeles Dodgers	4–0
1967	St. Louis Cardinals	Boston Red Sox	4–3
1968	Detroit Tigers	St. Louis Cardinals	4–3
1969	New York Mets	Baltimore Orioles	4–1
1970	Baltimore Orioles	Cincinnati Reds	4–1
1971	Pittsburgh Pirates	Baltimore Orioles	4–3
1972	Oakland Athletics	Cincinnati Reds	4–3
1973	Oakland Athletics	New York Mets	4–3
1974	Oakland Athletics	Los Angeles Dodgers	4–1
1975	Cincinnati Reds	Boston Red Sox	4–3
1976	Cincinnati Reds	New York Yankees	4–0
1977	New York Yankees	Los Angeles Dodgers	4–2
1978	New York Yankees	Los Angeles Dodgers	4–2
1979	Pittsburgh Pirates	Baltimore Orioles	4–3
1980	Philadelphia Phillies	Kansas City Royals	4–2
1981	Los Angeles Dodgers	New York Yankees	4–2
1982	St. Louis Cardinals	Milwaukee Brewers	4–3
1983	Baltimore Orioles	Philadelphia Phillies	4–1
1984	Detroit Tigers	San Diego Padres	4–1
1985	Kansas City Royals	St. Louis Cardinals	4–3
1986	New York Mets	Boston Red Sox	4–3
1987	Minnesota Twins	St. Louis Cardinals	4–3
1988	Los Angeles Dodgers	Oakland Athletics	4–1
1989	Oakland	San Francisco	4–0
1990	Cincinnati	Oakland	4–0
1991	Minnesota	Atlanta	4–3
1992	Toronto	Atlanta	4–2
1993	Toronto	Philadelphia	4–2
1993	Toronto	Philadelphia	4–2
1994	No series due to players' strike		
1995	Atlanta	Cleveland	4–2
1996	New York Yankees	Atlanta	4–2

1997	Florida	Cleveland	4–3
1998	New York Yankees	San Diego	4–0
1999	New York Yankees	Atlanta	4–0
2000	New York Yankees	New York Mets	4–1
2001	Arizona Diamondbacks	New York Yankees	4–3
2002	Anaheim Angels	San Francisco Giants	4–3
2003	Florida Marlins	New York Yankees	4–2
2004	Boston Red Sox	St. Louis Cardinals	4–0
2005	Chicago White Sox	Houston Astros	4–0
2006	St. Louis Cardinals	Detroit Tigers	4–1
2007	Boston Red Sox	Colorado Rockies	4–0
2008	Philadelphia Phillies	Tampa Bay Rays	4–1
2009	New York Yankees	Philadelphia Phillies	4–2

Quickies

Did you know ...

- that Reggie Jackson is the only player to win the World Series Most Valuable Player Award with two different teams? He won as a member of the 1973 Oakland Athletics and the 1977 New York Yankees.

American League Championship Series Results

Year	Winners	Finalists	Result
1969	Baltimore Orioles	Minnesota Twins	3–0
1970	Baltimore Orioles	Minnesota Twins	3–0
1971	Baltimore Orioles	Oakland Athletics	3–0
1972	Oakland Athletics	Detroit Tigers	3–2
1973	Oakland Athletics	Baltimore Orioles	3–2
1974	Oakland Athletics	Baltimore Orioles	3–0
1975	Boston Red Sox	Oakland Athletics	3–0
1976	New York Yankees	Kansas City Royals	3–2
1977	New York Yankees	Kansas City Royals	3–2
1978	New York Yankees	Kansas City Royals	3–1

1979	Baltimore Orioles	California Angels	3–1
1980	Kansas City Royals	New York Yankees	3–0
1981	New York Yankees	Oakland Athletics	3–0
1982	Milwaukee Brewers	California Angels	3–2
1983	Baltimore Orioles	Chicago White Sox	3–0
1984	Detroit Tigers	Kansas City Royals	3–0
1985	Kansas City Royals	Toronto Blue Jays	4–3
1986	Boston Red Sox	California Angels	4–3
1987	Minnesota Twins	Detroit Tigers	4–1
1988	Oakland Athletics	Boston Red Sox	4–0
1989	Oakland Athletics	Toronto Blue Jays	4–1
1990	Oakland Athletics	Boston Red Sox	4–0
1991	Minnesota Twins	Toronto Blue Jays	4–1
1992	Toronto Blue Jays	Oakland Athletics	4–2
1993	Toronto Blue Jays	Chicago White Sox	4–2
1994	No series due to players' strike		
1995	Cleveland Indians	Seattle Mariners	4–2
1996	New York Yankees	Baltimore Orioles	4–1
1997	Cleveland Indians	Baltimore Orioles	4–2
1998	New York Yankees	Cleveland Indians	4–2
1999	New York Yankees	Boston Red Sox	4–1
2000	New York Yankees	Seattle Mariners	4–2
2001	New York Yankees	Seattle Mariners	4–1
2002	Anaheim Angels	Minnesota Twins	4–1
2003	New York Yankees	Boston Red Sox	4–3
2004	Boston Red Sox	New York Yankees	4–3
2005	Chicago White Sox	Anaheim Angels	4–1
2006	Detroit Tigers	Oakland Athletics	4–0
2007	Boston Red Sox	Cleveland Indians	4–3
2008	Tampa Bay Rays	Boston Red Sox	4–3
2009	New York Yankees	Los Angeles Angels of Anaheim	4–2

National League Championship Series Results

Year	Winners	Finalists	Result
1969	New York Mets	Atlanta Braves	3–0
1970	Cincinnati Reds	Pittsburgh Pirates	3–0
1971	Pittsburgh Pirates	San Francisco Giants	3–1
1972	Cincinnati Reds	Pittsburgh Pirates	3–2
1973	New York Mets	Cincinnati Reds	3–2
1974	Los Angeles Dodgers	Pittsburgh Pirates	3–1
1975	Cincinnati Reds	Pittsburgh Pirates	3–0
1976	Cincinnati Reds	Philadelphia Phillies	3–0
1977	Los Angeles Dodgers	Philadelphia Phillies	3–1
1978	Los Angeles Dodgers	Philadelphia Phillies	3–1
1979	Pittsburgh Pirates	Cincinnati Reds	3–0
1980	Philadelphia Phillies	Houston Astros	3–2
1981	Los Angeles Dodgers	Montreal Expos	3–2
1982	St. Louis Cardinals	Atlanta Braves	3–0
1983	Philadelphia Phillies	Los Angeles Dodgers	3–1
1984	San Diego Padres	Chicago Cubs	3–2
1985	St. Louis Cardinals	Los Angeles Dodgers	4–2
1986	New York Mets	Houston Astros	4–2
1987	St. Louis Cardinals	San Francisco Giants	4–3
1988	Los Angeles Dodgers	New York Mets	4–3
1989	San Francisco Giants	Chicago Cubs	4–1
1990	Cincinnati Reds	Pittsburgh Pirates	4–2
1991	Atlanta Braves	Pittsburgh Pirates	4–3
1992	Atlanta Braves	Pittsburgh Pirates	4–3
1993	Philadelphia Phillies	Atlanta Braves	4–2

1994	No series due to players' strike		
1995	Atlanta Braves	Cincinnati Reds	4–0
1996	Atlanta Braves	St. Louis Cardinals	4–3
1997	Florida Marlins	Atlanta Braves	4–2
1998	San Diego Padres	Atlanta Braves	4–2
1999	Atlanta Braves	New York Mets	4–2
2000	New York Mets	St. Louis Cardinals	4–1
2001	Arizona Diamondbacks	Atlanta Braves	4–1
2002	San Francisco Giants	St. Louis Cardinals	4–1
2003	Florida Marlins	Chicago Cubs	4–3
2004	St. Louis Cardinals	Houston Astros	4–3
2005	Houston Astros	St. Louis Cardinals	4–2
2006	St. Louis Cardinals	New York Mets	4–3
2007	Colorado Rockies	Arizona Diamondbacks	4–0
2008	Philadelphia Phillies	Los Angeles Dodgers	4–1
2009	Philadelphia Phillies	Los Angeles Dodgers	4–1

Cy Young Award Winners

(Prior to 1967, one Cy Young Award winner represented both leagues)

Year	Player	Team	League
1956	Don Newcombe	Brooklyn Dodgers	
1957	Warren Spahn	Milwaukee Braves	
1958	Bob Turley	New York Yankees	
1959	Early Wynn	Chicago White Sox	
1960	Vernon Law	Pittsburgh Pirates	
1961	Whitey Ford	New York Yankees	
1962	Don Drysdale	Los Angeles Dodgers	
1963	Sandy Koufax	Los Angeles Dodgers	
1964	Dean Chance	California Angels	
1965	Sandy Koufax	Los Angeles Dodgers	
1966	Sandy Koufax	Los Angeles Dodgers	

1967	Mike McCormick	San Francisco Giants	NL
	Jim Lonborg	Boston Red Sox	AL
1968	Bob Gibson	St. Louis Cardinals	NL
	Dennis McLain	Detroit Tigers	AL
1969	Tom Seaver	New York Mets	NL
	Dennis McLain	Detroit Tigers	AL
	Mike Cuellar	Baltimore Orioles	AL
1970	Bob Gibson	St. Louis Cardinals	NL
	Jim Perry	Minnesota Twins	AL
1971	Ferguson Jenkins	Chicago Cubs	NL
	Vida Blue	Oakland Athletics	AL
1972	Steve Carlton	Philadelphia Phillies	NL
	Gaylord Perry	Cleveland Indians	AL
1973	Tom Seaver	New York Mets	NL
	Jim Palmer	Baltimore Orioles	AL
1974	Mike Marshall	Los Angeles Dodgers	NL
	Jim "Catfish" Hunter	Oakland Athletics	AL
1975	Tom Seaver	New York Mets	NL
	Jim Palmer	Baltimore Orioles	AL
1976	Randy Jones	San Diego Padres	NL
	Jim Palmer	Baltimore Orioles	AL
1977	Steve Carlton	Philadelphia Phillies	NL
	Sparky Lyle	New York Yankees	AL
1978	Gaylord Perry	San Diego Padres	NL
	Ron Guidry	New York Yankees	AL
1979	Bruce Sutter	Chicago Cubs	NL
	Mike Flanagan	Baltimore Orioles	AL
1980	Steve Carlton	Philadelphia Phillies	NL
	Steve Stone	Baltimore Orioles	AL
1981	Fernando Valenzuela	Los Angeles Dodgers	NL
	Rollie Fingers	Milwaukee Brewers	AL
1982	Steve Carlton	Philadelphia Phillies	NL
	Pete Vuckovich	Milwaukee Brewers	AL

1983	John Denny	Philadelphia Phillies	NL
	LaMarr Hoyt	Chicago White Sox	AL
1984	Rick Sutcliffe	Chicago Cubs	NL
	Willie Hernandez	Detroit Tigers	AL
1985	Dwight Gooden	New York Mets	NL
	Bret Saberhagen	Kansas City Royals	AL
1986	Mike Scott	Houston Astros	NL
	Roger Clemens	Boston Red Sox	AL
1987	Steve Bedrosian	Philadelphia Phillies	NL
	Roger Clemens	Boston Red Sox	AL
1988	Orel Hershiser	Los Angeles Dodgers	NL
	Frank Viola	Minnesota Twins	AL
1989	Mark Davis	San Diego Padres	NL
	Bret Saberhagen	Kansas City Royals	AL
1990	Doug Drabek	Pittsburgh Pirates	NL
	Bob Welch	Oakland Athletics	AL
1991	Tom Glavine	Atlanta Braves	NL
	Roger Clemens	Boston Red Sox	AL
1992	Greg Maddux	Chicago Cubs	NL
	Dennis Eckersley	Oakland Athletics	AL
1993	Greg Maddux	Atlanta Braves	NL
	Jack McDowell	Chicago White Sox	AL
1994	Greg Maddux	Atlanta Braves	NL
	David Cone	Kansas City Royals	AL
1995	Greg Maddux	Atlanta Braves	NL
	Randy Johnson	Seattle Mariners	AL
1996	John Smoltz	Atlanta Braves	NL
	Pat Hentgen	Toronto Blue Jays	AL
1997	Pedro Martinez	Montreal Expos	NL
	Roger Clemens	Toronto Blue Jays	AL
1998	Tom Glavine	Atlanta Braves	NL
	Roger Clemens	Toronto Blue Jays	AL
1999	Randy Johnson	Arizona Diamondbacks	NL

	Pedro Martinez	Boston Red Sox	AL
2000	Randy Johnson	Arizona Diamondbacks	NL
	Pedro Martinez	Boston Red Sox	AL
2001	Randy Johnson	Arizona Diamondbacks	NL
	Roger Clemens	New York Yankees	AL
2002	Randy Johnson	Arizona Diamondbacks	NL
	Barry Zito	Oakland Athletics	AL
2003	Eric Gagne	Los Angeles Dodgers	NL
	Roy Halladay	Toronto Blue Jays	AL
2004	Roger Clemens	Houston Astros	NL
	Johan Santana	Minnesota Twins	AL
2005	Chris Carpenter	St. Louis Cardinals	NL
	Bartolo Colon	Los Angeles Angels of Anaheim	AL
2006	Brandon Webb	Arizona Diamondbacks	NL
	Johan Santana	Minnesota Twins	AL
2007	Jake Peavy	San Diego Padres	NL
	C.C. Sabathia	Cleveland Indians	AL
2008	Tim Lincecum	San Francisco Giants	NL
	Cliff Lee	Cleveland Indians	AL
2009	Tim Lincecum	San Francisco Giants	NL
	Zack Greinke	Kansas City Royals	AL

Most Valuable Player Award Winners — American League

Year	Player	Team	Position
1931	Lefty Grove	Philadelphia Athletics	P
1932	Jimmie Foxx	Philadelphia Athletics	1B
1933	Jimmie Foxx	Philadelphia Athletics	1B
1934	Mickey Cochrane	Detroit Tigers	C
1935	Hank Greenberg	Detroit Tigers	1B
1936	Lou Gehrig	New York Yankees	1B
1937	Charlie Gehringer	Detroit Tigers	2B

1938	Jimmie Foxx	Boston Red Sox	1B
1939	Joe DiMaggio	New York Yankees	OF
1940	Hank Greenberg	Detroit Tigers	OF
1941	Joe DiMaggio	New York Yankees	OF
1942	Joe Gordon	New York Yankees	2B
1943	Spud Chandler	New York Yankees	P
1944	Hal Newhouser	Detroit Tigers	P
1945	Hal Newhouser	Detroit Tigers	P
1946	Ted Williams	Boston Red Sox	OF
1947	Joe DiMaggio	New York Yankees	OF
1948	Lou Boudreau	Cleveland Indians	SS
1949	Ted Williams	Boston Red Sox	OF
1950	Phil Rizzuto	New York Yankees	SS
1951	Yogi Berra	New York Yankees	C
1952	Bobby Shantz	Philadelphia Athletics	P
1953	Al Rosen	Cleveland Indians	3B
1954	Yogi Berra	New York Yankees	C
1955	Yogi Berra	New York Yankees	C
1956	Mickey Mantle	New York Yankees	OF
1957	Mickey Mantle	New York Yankees	OF
1958	Jackie Jensen	Boston Red Sox	OF
1959	Nellie Fox	Chicago White Sox	2B
1960	Roger Maris	New York Yankees	OF
1961	Roger Maris	New York Yankees	OF
1962	Mickey Mantle	New York Yankees	OF
1963	Elston Howard	New York Yankees	C
1964	Brooks Robinson	Baltimore Orioles	3B
1965	Zoilo Versalles	Minnesota Twins	SS
1966	Frank Robinson	Baltimore Orioles	OF
1967	Carl Yastrzemski	Boston Red Sox	OF
1968	Denny McLain	Detroit Tigers	P
1969	Harmon Killebrew	Minnesota Twins	1B/3B
1970	Boog Powell	Baltimore Orioles	1B

1971	Vida Blue	Oakland Athletics	P
1972	Richie Allen	Chicago White Sox	1B
1973	Reggie Jackson	Oakland Athletics	OF
1974	Jeff Burroughs	Texas Rangers	OF
1975	Fred Lynn	Boston Red Sox	OF
1976	Thurman Munson	New York Yankees	C
1977	Rod Carew	Minnesota Twins	1B
1978	Jim Rice	Boston Red Sox	OF
1979	Don Baylor	California Angels	OF
1980	George Brett	Kansas City Royals	3B
1981	Rollie Fingers	Milwaukee Brewers	P
1982	Robin Yount	Milwaukee Brewers	SS
1983	Cal Ripken, Jr.	Baltimore Orioles	SS
1984	Willie Hernandez	Detroit Tigers	P
1985	Don Mattingly	New York Yankees	1B
1986	Roger Clemens	Boston Red Sox	P
1987	George Bell	Toronto Blue Jays	OF
1988	Jose Canseco	Oakland Athletics	OF
1989	Robin Yount	Milwaukee Brewers	OF
1990	Rickey Henderson	Oakland Athletics	OF
1991	Cal Ripken, Jr.	Baltimore Orioles	SS
1992	Dennis Eckersley	Oakland Athletics	P
1993	Frank Thomas	Chicago White Sox	1B
1994	Frank Thomas	Chicago White Sox	1B
1995	Mo Vaughn	Boston Red Sox	1B
1996	Juan Gonzalez	Texas Rangers	OF
1997	Ken Griffey, Jr.	Seattle Mariners	OF
1998	Juan Gonzalez	Texas Rangers	OF
1999	Ivan Rodriguez	Texas Rangers	C
2000	Jason Giambi	Oakland Athletics	1B
2001	Ichiro Suzuki	Seattle Mariners	RF
2002	Miguel Tejada	Oakland Athletics	SS
2003	Alex Rodriguez	Texas Rangers	SS

2004	Vladimir Guerrero	Anaheim Angels	RF
2005	Alex Rodriguez,	New York Yankees	3B
2006	Justin Morneau	Minnesota Twins	1B
2007	Alex Rodriguez	New York Yankees	3B
2008	Dustin Pedroia	Boston Red Sox	2B
2009	Joe Mauer	Minnesota Twins	C

Most Valuable Player Award Winners — National League

Year	Player	Team	Position
1931	Frankie Frisch	Chicago Cubs	2B
1932	Chuck Klein	Philadelphia Phillies	LF
1933	Carl Hubbell	New York Giants	P
1934	Dizzy Dean	St. Louis Cardinals	P
1935	Gabby Hartnett	Chicago Cubs	C
1936	Carl Hubbell	New York Giants	P
1937	Joe Medwick	St. Louis Cardinals	RF
1938	Ernie Lombardi	Cincinnati Reds	C
1939	Bucky Walters	Cincinnati Reds	P
1940	Frank McCormick	Cincinnati Reds	1B
1941	Dolph Camilli	Brooklyn Dodgers	1B
1942	Mort Cooper	St. Louis Cardinals	P
1943	Stan Musial	St. Louis Cardinals	1B/OF
1944	Marty Marion	St. Louis Cardinals	SS
1945	Phil Cavarretta	Chicago Cubs	1B
1946	Stan Musial	St. Louis Cardinals	1B/OF
1947	Bob Elliott	Boston Braves	3B
1948	Stan Musial	St. Louis Cardinals	LF
1949	Jackie Robinson	Brookyln Dodgers	2B
1950	Jim Kostanty	Philadelphia Phillies	P
1951	Roy Campanella	Brooklyn Dodgers	C
1952	Hank Sauer	Chicago Cubs	LF

1953	Roy Campanella	Brooklyn Dodgers	C
1954	Willie Mays	New York Giants	CF
1955	Roy Campanella	Brooklyn Dodgers	C
1956	Don Newcombe	Brooklyn Dodgers	P
1957	Hank Aaron	Milwaukee Braves	RF
1958	Ernie Banks	Chicago Cubs	SS
1959	Ernie Banks	Chicago Cubs	SS
1960	Dick Groat	Pittsburgh Pirates	SS
1961	Frank Robinson	Cincinnati Reds	LF
1962	Maury Wills	Los Angeles Dodgers	SS
1963	Sandy Koufax	Los Angeles Dodgers	P
1964	Ken Boyer	St. Louis Cardinals	3B
1965	Willie Mays	San Francisco Giants	CF
1966	Roberto Clemente	Pittsburgh Pirates	LF
1967	Orlando Cepeda	St. Louis Cardinals	1B
1968	Bob Gibson	St. Louis Cardinals	P
1969	Willie McCovey	San Francisco Giants	1B
1970	Johnny Bench	Cincinnati Reds	C
1971	Joe Torre	St. Louis Cardinals	3B
1972	Johnny Bench	Cincinnati Reds	C
1973	Pete Rose	Cincinnati Reds	RF
1974	Steve Garvey	Los Angeles Dodgers	1B
1975	Joe Morgan	Cincinnati Reds	2B
1976	Joe Morgan	Cincinnati Reds	2B
1977	George Foster	Cincinnati Reds	LF
1978	Dave Parker	Pittsburgh Pirates	RF
1979	Willie Stargell	Pittsburgh Pirates	1B
1979	Keith Hernandez	New York Mets	1B
1980	Mike Schmidt	Philadelphia Phillies	3B
1981	Mike Schmidt	Philadelphia Phillies	3B
1982	Dale Murphy	Atlanta Braves	LF
1983	Dale Murphy	Atlanta Braves	LF
1984	Ryne Sandberg	Chicago Cubs	2B

1985	Willie McGee	St. Louis Cardinals	CF
1986	Mike Schmidt	Philadelphia Phillies	3B
1987	Andre Dawson	Chicago Cubs	LF
1988	Kirk Gibson	Los Angeles Dodgers	LF
1989	Kevin Mitchell	San Francisco Giants	RF
1990	Barry Bonds	Pittsburgh Pirates	LF
1991	Terry Pendleton	Atlanta Braves	3B
1992	Barry Bonds	San Francisco Giants	LF
1993	Barry Bonds	San Francisco Giants	LF
1994	Jeff Bagwell	Houston Astros	1B
1995	Barry Larkin	Cincinnati Reds	SS
1996	Ken Caminiti	San Diego Padres	3B
1997	Larry Walker	Colorado Rockies	RF
1998	Sammy Sosa	Chicago Cubs	RF
1999	Chipper Jones	Atlanta Braves	3B
2000	Jeff Kent	San Francisco Giants	2B
2001	Barry Bonds	San Francisco Giants	LF
2002	Barry Bonds	San Francisco Giants	LF
2003	Barry Bonds	San Francisco Giants	LF
2004	Barry Bonds	San Francisco Giants	LF
2005	Albert Pujols	St. Louis Cardinals	1B
2006	Ryan Howard	Philadelphia Phillies	1B
2007	Jimmy Rollins	Philadelphia Phillies	SS
2008	Albert Pujols	St. Louis Cardinals	1B
2009	Albert Pujols	St. Louis Cardinals	1B

World Series Most Valuable Players

Year	Player	Team	League
1955	Johnny Podres	Brooklyn Dodgers	NL
1956	Don Larsen	New York Yankees	AL
1957	Lew Burdette	Milwaukee Braves	NL

1958	Bob Turley	New York Yankees	AL
1959	Larry Sherry	Los Angeles Dodgers	NL
1960	Bobby Richardson	New York Yankees	AL
1961	Whitey Ford	New York Yankees	AL
1962	Ralph Terry	New York Yankees	AL
1963	Sandy Koufax	Los Angeles Dodgers	NL
1964	Bob Gibson	St. Louis Cardinals	NL
1965	Sandy Koufax	Los Angeles Dodgers	NL
1966	Frank Robinson	Baltimore Orioles	AL
1967	Bob Gibson	St. Louis Cardinals	NL
1968	Mickey Lolich	Detroit Tigers	AL
1969	Donn Clendenon	New York Mets	NL
1970	Brooks Robinson	Baltimore Orioles	AL
1971	Roberto Clemente	Pittsburgh Pirates	NL
1972	Gene Tenace	Oakland Athletics	NL
1973	Reggie Jackson	Oakland Athletics	NL
1974	Rollie Fingers	Oakland Athletics	NL
1975	Pete Rose	Cincinnati Reds	NL
1976	Johnny Bench	Cincinnati Reds	NL
1977	Reggie Jackson	New York Yankees	AL
1978	Bucky Dent	New York Yankees	AL
1979	Willie Stargell	Pittsburgh Pirates	NL
1980	Mike Schmidt	Philadelphia Phillies	NL
1981	Ron Cey, Pedro Guerrero, and Steve Yeager	Los Angeles Dodgers	NL
1982	Darrell Porter	St. Louis Cardinals	NL
1983	Rick Dempsey	Baltimore Orioles	AL
1984	Alan Trammell	Detroit Tigers	AL
1985	Bret Saberhagen	Kansas City Royals	AL
1986	Ray Knight	New York Mets	NL
1987	Frank Viola	Minnesota Twins	AL
1988	Orel Hershiser	Los Angeles Dodgers	NL

1989	Dave Stewart	Oakland Athletics	NL
1990	Jose Rijo	Cincinnati Reds	NL
1991	Jack Morris	Minnesota Twins	AL
1992	Pat Borders	Toronto Blue Jays	AL
1993	Paul Molitor	Toronto Blue Jays	AL
1994	No series due to players' strike.		
1995	Tom Glavine	Atlanta Braves	NL
1996	John Wetteland	New York Yankees	AL
1997	Livan Hernandez	Florida Marlins	NL
1998	Scott Brosius	New York Yankees	AL
1999	Mariano Rivera	New York Yankees	AL
2000	Derek Jeter	New York Yankees	AL
2001	Curt Schilling and Randy Johnson	Arizona Diamondbacks	NL
2002	Troy Glaus	Anaheim Angels	AL
2003	Josh Beckett	Florida Marlins	NL
2004	Manny Ramirez	Boston Red Sox	AL
2005	Jermaine Dye	Chicago White Sox	AL
2006	David Eckstein	St. Louis Cardinals	NL
2007	Mike Lowell	Boston Red Sox	AL
2008	Cole Hamels	Philadelphia Phillies	NL
2009	Hideki Matsui	New York Yankees	AL

Playoff Dominance: The Only Five Men to Win an LCS and World Series MVP Award in the Same Year

Year	Player	Team
1979	Willie Stargell	Pittsburgh Pirates
1982	Darrell Porter	St. Louis Cardinals
1988	Orel Hershizer	Los Angeles Dodgers
1998	Livan Hernandez	Florida Marlins
2008	Cole Hamels	Philadelphia Phillies

American League Championship
Series Most Valuable Players

Year	Player	Team
1980	Frank White	Kansas City Royals
1981	Graig Nettles	New York Yankees
1982	Fred Lynn	California Angels
1983	Mike Boddicker	Baltimore Orioles
1984	Kirk Gibson	Detroit Tigers
1985	George Brett	Kansas City Royals
1986	Marty Barrett	Boston Red Sox
1987	Gary Gaetti	Minnesota Twins
1988	Dennis Eckersley	Oakland A's
1989	Rickey Henderson	Oakland A's
1990	Dave Stewart	Oakland A's
1991	Kirby Puckett	Minnesota Twins
1992	Roberto Alomar	Toronto Blue Jays
1993	Dave Stewart	Toronto Blue Jays
1994	No series due to players' strike	
1995	Orel Hershiser	Cleveland Indians
1996	Bernie Williams	New York Yankees
1997	Marquis Grissom	Cleveland Indians
1998	David Wells	New York Yankees
1999	Orlando Hernandez	New York Yankees
2000	David Justice	New York Yankees
2001	Andy Pettitte	New York Yankees
2002	Adam Kennedy	Anaheim Angels
2003	Mariano Rivera	New York Yankees
2004	David Ortiz	Boston Red Sox
2005	Paul Konerko	Chicago White Sox
2006	Placido Polanco	Detroit Tigers
2007	Josh Beckett	Boston Red Sox
2008	Matt Garza	Tampa Bay Rays
2009	C.C. Sabathia	New York Yankees

National League Championship Series Most Valuable Players

Year	Player	Team
1977	Dusty Baker	Los Angeles Dodgers
1978	Steve Garvey	Los Angeles Dodgers
1979	Willie Stargell	Pittsburgh Pirates
1980	Manny Trillo	Philadelphia Phillies
1981	Burt Hooton	Los Angeles Dodgers
1982	Darrell Porter	St. Louis Cardinals
1983	Gary Matthews	Philadelphia Phillies
1984	Steve Garvey	San Diego Padres
1985	Ozzie Smith	St. Louis Cardinals
1986	Mike Scott	Houston Astros
1987	Jeffrey Leonard	San Francisco Giants
1988	Orel Hershiser	Los Angeles Dodgers
1989	Will Clark	San Francisco Giants
1990	Rob Dibble and Randy Myers	Cincinnati Reds
1991	Steve Avery	Atlanta Braves
1992	John Smoltz	Atlanta Braves
1993	Curt Schilling	Philadelphia Phillies
1994	No series due to players' strike	
1995	Mike Devereaux	Atlanta Braves
1996	Javy Lopez	Atlanta Braves
1997	Livan Hernandez	Florida Marlins
1998	Sterling Hitchcock	San Diego Padres
1999	Eddie Perez	Atlanta Braves
2000	Mike Hampton	New York Mets
2001	Craig Counsell	Arizona Diamondbacks
2002	Benito Santiago	San Francisco Giants
2003	Ivan Rodriguez	Florida Marlins
2004	Albert Pujols	St. Louis Cardinals
2005	Roy Oswalt	Houston Astros
2006	Jeff Suppan	St. Louis Cardinals

2007	Matt Holliday	Colorado Rockies
2008	Cole Hamels	Philadelphia Phillies
2009	Ryan Howard	Philadelphia Phillies

Major League Baseball All-Star Game Results

Year	Stadium	League	Result
1933	Comiskey Park, Chicago	American	4–2
1934	Polo Grounds, New York	American	9–7
1935	Municipal Stadium, Cleveland	American	4–1
1936	Braves Field, Boston	National	4–3
1937	Griffith Stadium, Washington	American	8–3
1938	Crosley Field, Cincinnati	National	4–1
1939	Yankee Stadium, New York	American	3–1
1940	Sportsman's Park, St. Louis	National	4–0
1941	Briggs Stadium, Detroit	American	7–5
1942	Polo Grounds, New York	American	3–1
1943	Shibe Park, Philadelphia	American	5–3
1944	Forbes Field, Pittsburgh	National	7–1
1945	No game held		
1946	Fenway Park, Boston	American	12–0
1947	Wrigley Field, Chicago	American	2–1
1948	Sportsman's Park, St. Louis	American	5–2
1949	Ebbets Field, Brooklyn	American	11–7
1950	Comiskey Park, Chicago	National	4–3
1951	Briggs Stadium, Detroit	National	8–3
1952	Shibe Park, Philadelphia	National	3–2
1953	Crosley Field, Cincinnati	National	5–1
1954	Municipal Stadium, Cleveland	American	11–9
1955	County Stadium, Milwaukee	National	6–5
1956	Griffith Stadium, Washington	National	7–3
1957	Sportsman's Park, St. Louis	American	6–5

1958	Memorial Stadium, Baltimore	American	4–3
1959	Forbes Field, Pittsburgh	National	5–4
1959	Memorial Coliseum, Los Angeles	American	5–3
1960	Municipal Stadium, Kansas City	National	5–3
	Yankee Stadium, New York	National	6–0
1961	Candlestick Park, San Francisco	National	5–4
	Fenway Park, Boston		Tie 1–1
1962	D.C. Stadium, Washington	National	3–1
	Wrigley Field, Chicago	American	9–4
1963	Municipal Stadium, Cleveland	National	5–3
1964	Shea Stadium, New York	National	7–4
1965	Metropolitan Stadium, Bloomington, Minnesota	National	6–5
1966	Busch Memorial Stadium, St. Louis	National	2–1
1967	Anaheim Stadium, Anaheim, California	National	2–1
1968	Astrodome, Houston	National	1–0
1969	RFK Memorial Stadium, Washington, D.C.	National	9–3
1970	Riverfront Stadium, Cincinnati	National	5–4
1971	Tiger Stadium, Detroit	American	6–4
1972	Atlanta–Fulton County Stadium, Atlanta	National	4–3
1973	Royals Stadium, Kansas City	National	7–1
1974	Three Rivers Stadium, Pittsburgh	National	7–2
1975	County Stadium, Milwaukee	National	6–3
1976	Veterans Stadium, Philadelphia	National	7–1
1977	Yankee Stadium, New York	National	7–5
1978	San Diego Stadium	National	7–3
1979	Kingdome, Seattle	National	7–6
1980	Dodger Stadium, Los Angeles	National	4–2
1981	Municipal Stadium, Cleveland	National	5–4
1982	Olympic Stadium, Montreal	National	4–1

1983	Comiskey Park, Chicago	American	13–3
1984	Candlestick Park, San Francisco	National	3–1
1985	H. Humphrey Metrodome, Minneapolis	National	6–1
1986	Astrodome, Houston	American	3–2
1987	Oakland–Alameda County Stadium, Oakland	National	2–0
1988	Riverfront Stadium, Cincinnati	American	2–1
1989	Anaheim Stadium, Anaheim	American	5–3
1990	Wrigley Field, Chicago	American	2–0
1991	SkyDome, Toronto	American	4–2
1992	Jack Murphy Stadium, San Diego	American	13–6
1993	Oriole Park at Camden Yards, Baltimore	American	9–3
1994	Three Rivers Stadium, Pittsburgh	National	8–7
1995	The Ballpark at Arlington, Texas	National	3–2
1996	Veterans Stadium, Philadelphia	National	6–0
1997	Jacobs Field, Cleveland	American	3–1
1998	Coors Field, Denver	American	13–8
1999	Fenway Park, Boston	American	4–1
2000	Turner Field, Atlanta	American	6–3
2001	SAFECO Field, Seattle	American	4–1
2002	Miller Park, Milwaukee		Tie 7–7
2003	U.S. Cellular Field, Chicago	American	7–6
2004	Minute Maid Park, Houston	American	9–4
2005	Comerica Park, Detroit	American	7–5
2006	PNC Park, Pittsburgh	American	3–2
2007	AT&T Park, San Francisco	American	5–4
2008	Yankee Stadium, New York	American	4–3
2009	Busch Stadium, St. Louis	American	4–3

Major League Baseball Rookie of the Year Award Winners

Year	Player	Team	League
1947*	Jackie Robinson	Brooklyn Dodgers	
1948*	Alvin Dark	Boston Braves	
1949	Don Newcombe	Brooklyn Dodgers	NL
	Roy Sievers	St. Louis Browns	AL
1950	Sam Jethroe	Boston Braves	NL
	Walt Dropo	Boston Red Sox	AL
1951	Willie Mays	New York Giants	NL
	Gil McDougald	New York Yankees	AL
1952	Joe Black	Brooklyn Dodgers	NL
	Harry Byrd	Philadelphia Athletics	AL
1953	Jim Gilliam	Brooklyn Dodgers	NL
	Harvey Kuenn	Detroit Tigers	AL
1954	Wally Moon	St. Louis Cardinals	NL
	Bob Grim	New York Yankees	AL
1955	Bill Virdon	St. Louis Cardinals	NL
	Herb Score	Cleveland Indians	AL
1956	Frank Robinson	Cincinnati Reds	NL
	Luis Aparicio	Chicago White Sox	AL
1957	Jack Sanford	Philadelphia Phillies	NL
	Tony Kubek	New York Yankees	AL
1958	Orlando Cepeda	San Francisco Giants	NL
	Albie Pearson	Washington Senators	AL
1959	Willie McCovey	San Francisco Giants	NL
	Bob Allison	Washington Senators	AL
1960	Frank Howard	Los Angeles Dodgers	NL
	Ron Hansen	Baltimore Orioles	AL
1961	Billy Williams	Chicago Cubs	NL
	Don Schwall	Boston Red Sox	AL
1962	Ken Hubbs	Chicago Cubs	NL
	Tom Tresh	New York Yankees	AL

1963	Pete Rose	Cincinnati Reds	NL
	Gary Peters	Chicago White Sox	AL
1964	Richie Allen	Philadelphia Phillies	NL
	Tony Oliva	Minnesota Twins	AL
1965	Jim Lefebvre	Los Angeles Dodgers	NL
	Curt Blefary	Baltimore Orioles	AL
1966	Tommy Helms	Cincinnati Reds	NL
	Tommie Agee	Chicago White Sox	AL
1967	Tom Seaver	New York Mets	NL
	Rod Carew	Minnesota Twins	AL
1968	Johnny Bench	Cincinnati Reds	NL
	Stan Bahnsen	New York Yankees	AL
1969	Ted Sizemore	Los Angeles Dodgers	NL
	Lou Piniella	Kansas City Royals	AL
1970	Carl Morton	Montreal Expos	NL
	Thurman Munson	New York Yankees	AL
1971	Earl Williams	Atlanta Braves	NL
	Chris Chambliss	Cleveland Indians	AL
1972	Jon Matlack	New York Mets	NL
	Carlton Fisk	Boston Red Sox	AL
1973	Gary Matthews	San Francisco Giants	NL
	Al Bumbry	Baltimore Orioles	AL
1974	Bake McBride	St. Louis Cardinals	NL
	Mike Hargrove	Texas Rangers	AL
1975	John Montefusco	San Francisco Giants	NL
	Fred Lynn	Boston Red Sox	AL
1976	Butch Metzger	Cincinnati Reds	NL
	Pat Zachry	San Diego Padres	NL
	Mark Fidrych	Detroit Tigers	AL
1977	Andre Dawson	Montreal Expos	NL
	Eddie Murray	Baltimore Orioles	AL
1978	Bob Horner	Atlanta Braves	NL
	Lou Whitaker	Detroit Tigers	AL

1979	Rick Sutcliffe	Los Angeles Dodgers	NL
	John Castino	Minnesota Twins	AL
	Alfredo Griffin	Toronto Blue Jays	AL
1980	Steve Howe	Los Angeles Dodgers	NL
	Joe Charboneau	Cleveland Indians	AL
1981	Fernando Valenzuela	Los Angeles Dodgers	NL
	Dave Righetti	New York Yankees	AL
1982	Steve Sax	Los Angeles Dodgers	NL
	Cal Ripken, Jr.	Baltimore Orioles	AL
1983	Darryl Strawberry	New York Mets	NL
	Ron Kittle	Chicago White Sox	AL
1984	Dwight Gooden	New York Mets	NL
	Alvin Davis	Seattle Mariners	AL
1985	Vince Coleman	St. Louis Cardinals	NL
	Ozzie Guillen	Chicago White Sox	AL
1986	Todd Worrell	St. Louis Cardinals	NL
	Jose Canseco	Oakland Athletics	AL
1987	Benito Santiago	San Diego Padres	NL
	Mark McGwire	Oakland Athletics	AL
1988	Chris Sabo	Cincinnati Reds	NL
	Walt Weiss	Oakland Athletics	AL
1989	Jerome Walton	Chicago Cubs	NL
	Gregg Olson	Baltimore Orioles	AL
1990	Dave Justice	Atlanta Braves	NL
	Sandy Alomar, Jr.	Cleveland Indians	AL
1991	Jeff Bagwell	Houston Astros	NL
	Chuck Knoblauch	Minnesota Twins	AL
1992	Eric Karros	Los Angeles Dodgers	NL
	Pat Listach	Milwaukee Brewers	AL
1993	Mike Piazza	Los Angeles Dodgers	NL
	Tim Salmon	California Angels	AL
1994	Raul Mondesi	Los Angeles Dodgers	NL
	Bob Hamelin	Kansas City Royals	AL

1995	Hideo Nomo	Los Angeles Dodgers	NL
	Marty Cordova	Minnesota Twins	AL
1996	Todd Hollandsworth	Los Angeles Dodgers	NL
	Derek Jeter	New York Yankees	AL
1997	Scott Rolen	Philadelphia Phillies	NL
	Nomar Garciaparra	Boston Red Sox	AL
1998	Kerry Wood	Chicago Cubs	NL
	Ben Grieve	Oakland Athletics	AL
1999	Scott Williamson	Cincinnati Reds	NL
	Carlos Beltran	Kansas City Athletics	AL
2000	Rafael Furcal	Atlanta Braves	NL
	Kazuhiro Sasaki	Seattle Mariners	AL
2001	Albert Pujols	St. Louis Cardinals	NL
	Ichiro Suzuki	Seattle Mariners	AL
2002	Jason Jennings	Colorado Rockies	NL
	Eric Hinske	Toronto Blue Jays	AL
2003	Dontrelle Willis	Florida Marlins	NL
	Angel Berroa	Kansas City Royals	AL
2004	Jason Bay	Pittsburgh Pirates	NL
	Bobby Crosby	Oakland Athletics	AL
2005	Ryan Howard	Philadelphia Phillies	NL
	Huston Street	Oakland Athletics	AL
2006	Hanley Ramirez	Florida Marlins	NL
	Justin Verlander	Detroit Tigers	AL
2007	Ryan Braun	Milwaukee Brewers	NL
	Dustin Pedroia	Boston Red Sox	AL
2008	Geovany Soto	Chicago Cubs	NL
	Evan Longoria	Tampa Bay Rays	AL
2009	Chris Coghlan	Florida Marlins	NL
	Andrew Bailey	Oakland Athletics	AL

*For two years, the Rookie of the Year Award was given for the outstanding rookie in all of baseball. The award was not divided by league until 1949.

Japan Series Results

Year	Winners	Finalists	Result
1950	Mainichi Orions (PL)	Shochiku Robins (CL)	4–2
1951	Yomiuri Giants (CL)	Nankai Hawks (PL)	4–1
1952	Yomiuri Giants (CL)	Nankai Hawks (PL)	4–2
1953	Yomiuri Giants (CL)	Nankai Hawks (PL)	4–2
1954	Chunichi Dragons (CL)	Nishitetsu Lions (PL)	4–3
1955	Yomiuri Giants (CL)	Nankai Hawks (PL)	4–3
1956	Nishitetsu Lions (PL)	Yomiuri Giants (CL)	4–2
1957	Nishitetsu Lions (PL)	Yomiuri Giants (CL)	4–0
1958	Nishitetsu Lions (PL)	Yomiuri Giants (CL)	4–3
1959	Nankai Hawks (PL)	Yomiuri Giants (CL)	4–0
1960	Taiyo Whales (CL)	Daimai Orions (PL)	4–0
1961	Yomiuri Giants (CL)	Nankai Hawks (PL)	4–2
1962	Toei Flyers (PL)	Hanshin Tigers (CL)	4–2
1963	Yomiuri Giants (CL)	Nishitetsu Lions (PL)	4–3
1964	Nankai Hawks (PL)	Hanshin Tigers (CL)	4–3
1965	Yomiuri Giants (CL)	Nankai Hawks (PL)	4–1
1966	Yomiuri Giants (CL)	Nankai Hawks (PL)	4–2
1967	Yomiuri Giants (CL)	Hankyu Braves (PL)	4–2
1968	Yomiuri Giants (CL)	Hankyu Braves (PL)	4–2
1969	Yomiuri Giants (CL)	Hankyu Braves (PL)	4–2
1970	Yomiuri Giants (CL)	Lotte Orions (PL)	4–1
1971	Yomiuri Giants (CL)	Hankyu Braves (PL)	4–1
1972	Yomiuri Giants (CL)	Hankyu Braves (PL)	4–1
1973	Yomiuri Giants (CL)	Nankai Hawks (PL)	4–1
1974	Lotte Orions (PL)	Chunichi Dragons (CL)	4–2
1975	Hankyu Braves (PL)	Hiroshima Toyo Carp (CL)	4–0
1976	Hankyu Braves (PL)	Yomiuri Giants (CL)	4–3
1977	Hankyu Braves (PL)	Yomiuri Giants (CL)	4–1
1978	Yakult Swallows (CL)	Hankyu Braves (PL)	4–3

1979	Hiroshima Toyo Carp (CL)	Kintetsu Buffaloes (PL)	4–3
1980	Hiroshima Toyo Carp (CL)	Kintetsu Buffaloes (PL)	4–3
1981	Yomiuri Giants (CL)	Nippon-Ham Fighters (PL)	4–2
1982	Seibu Lions (PL)	Chunichi Dragons (CL)	4–2
1983	Seibu Lions (PL)	Yomiuri Giants (CL)	4–3
1984	Hiroshima Toyo Carp (CL)	Hankyu Braves (PL)	4–3
1985	Hanshin Tigers (CL)	Seibu Lions (PL)	4–2
1986	Seibu Lions (PL)	Hiroshima Toyo Carp (CL)	4–3
1987	Seibu Lions (PL)	Yomiuri Giants (CL)	4–2
1988	Seibu Lions (PL)	Chunichi Dragons (CL)	4–1
1989	Yomiuri Giants (CL)	Kintetsu Buffaloes (PL)	4–3
1990	Seibu Lions (PL)	Yomiuri Giants (CL)	4–0
1991	Seibu Lions (PL)	Hiroshima Toyo Carp (CL)	4–3
1992	Seibu Lions (PL)	Yakult Swallows (CL)	4–3
1993	Yakult Swallows (CL)	Seibu Lions (PL)	4–3
1994	Yomiuri Giants (CL)	Seibu Lions (PL)	4–2
1995	Yakult Swallows (CL)	Orix BlueWave (PL)	4–1
1996	Orix BlueWave (PL)	Yomiuri Giants (CL)	4–1
1997	Yakult Swallows (CL)	Seibu Lions (PL)	4–1
1998	Yokohama BayStars (CL)	Seibu Lions (PL)	4–2
1999	Fukuoka Daiei Hawks (PL)	Chunichi Dragons (CL)	4–1
2000	Yomiuri Giants (CL)	Fukuoka Daiei Hawks (PL)	4–2
2001	Yakult Swallows (CL)	Osaka Kintetsu Buffaloes (PL)	4–1
2002	Yomiuri Giants (CL)	Seibu Lions (PL)	4–0

2003	Fukuoka Daiei Hawks (PL)	Hanshin Tigers (CL)	4–2
2004	Seibu Lions (PL)	Chunichi Dragons (CL)	4–3
2005	Chiba Lotte Marines (PL)	Hanshin Tigers (CL)	4–0
2006	Nippon-Ham Fighters (PL)	Chunichi Dragons (CL) 4–1	
2007	Chunichi Dragons (CL)	Nippon-Ham Fighters (PL) 4–1	
2008	Seibu Lions (PL)	Yomiuri Giants (CL) 4–3	
2009	Yomiuri Giants (CL)	Hokkaido Nippon Ham Fighters (PL)	4–2

World Baseball Classic Finals Results

Year	Winners	Finalists	Result
2006	Japan	South Korea	5–3
2009	Japan	Cuba	10–6

Negro National League vs. Eastern Coloured League

Year	Winners	Finalists	Result
1924	Kansas City Monarchs (NNL)	Hilldale Club (ECL)	5–4
1925	Hilldale Club (ECL)	Kansas City Monarchs (NNL)	5–1
1926	Chicago American Giants (NNL)	Bacharach Giants (ECL)	5–3
1927	Chicago American Giants (NNL)	Bacharach Giants (ECL)	5–3

Negro American League vs. Negro National League

Year	Winners	Finalists	Result
1942	Kansas City Monarchs (NAL)	Homestead Grays (NNL)	4–0
1943	Homestead Grays (NNL)	Birmingham Black Barons (NAL)	4–3
1944	Homestead Grays (NNL)	Birmingham Black Barons (NAL)	4–1
1945	Cleveland Buckeyes (NAL)	Homestead Grays (NNL)	4–0
1946	Newark Eagles (NNL)	Kansas City Monarchs (NAL)	4–3
1947	New York Cubans (NNL)	Cleveland Buckeyes (NAL)	4–1
1948	Homestead Grays (NNL)	Birmingham Black Barons (NAL)	4–1

question
and feature list

Baseball History

Stadiums

Fact or Fiction?

Rules and Lingo

Names

Baseball Media and Popular Culture

Plays, Strategies, and Statistics

Great Moments

Blunders, Jokes, and Not-So-Great Moments

Firsts and Record-Breakers

The Greats and Near-Greats

Traditions and Superstitions

The Best of the Best: Baseball's Thirty Most Memorable Moments

Champions and Award Winners

Other Books in the Now You Know Series

**Now You Know
Football**
978-1-55488-453-7
$19.99

**Now You Know
Soccer**
978-1-55002-416-2
$19.99

**Now You Know
Golf**
978-1-55002-870-6
$19.99

**Now You Know
Hockey**
978-1-55002-869-0
$19.99

**Now You Know
Big Book of Sports**
978-1-55488-454-4
$29.99

**Now You Know
Big Book of Answers 2**
978-1-55002-871-3
$29.99

More Books in the Now You Know Series

Available at your favourite bookseller.

DUNDURN PRESS
www.dundurn.com